THE FREELANCE BIBLE

ABOUT THE AUTHOR

Alison Grade is a career freelancer, serial entrepreneur and founder of the company Mission Accomplished, a consultancy that offers training, mentoring and strategic advice to start-ups and established SMEs principally in the creative industries. She is a NESTA-accredited creative enterprise trainer and has delivered international programmes in association with the British Council. She is the CEO of Screen Central which represents the professional screen community in the West Midlands where she lives.

THE FREELANCE BIBLE

EVERYTHING YOU NEED TO GO SOLO IN ANY INDUSTRY

Alison Grade

BUSINESS

PENGUIN BUSINESS

UK | USA | Canada | Ireland | Australia
India | New Zealand | South Africa

Penguin Business is part of the Penguin Random House group of companies whose addresses can be found at global.penguinrandomhouse.com.

First published 2020
001

Set in 12/14.75pt Dante MT Std
Typeset by Jouve (UK), Milton Keynes
Printed and bound in Great Britain by Clays Ltd, Elcograf S.p.A.

A CIP catalogue record for this book is available from the British Library

ISBN: 978-0-241-39948-4

Follow us on LinkedIn: linkedin.com/company/penguinbusiness

www.greenpenguin.co.uk

To Seán, Thomas and Alex

'That which costs little is less valued.'
Miguel de Cervantes, *The Life and Exploits of the Ingenious Gentleman Don Quixote de la Mancha*

CONTENTS

FREELANCING – CAREER CHOICE OR NECESSITY?

Do you have a real talent or skill you would love to turn into your own independent livelihood but find the idea of self-employment daunting? Do you need to be a freelancer in order to do the work you love?

I've been a freelancer for most of my career. It suits me, and is how I function best in the work environment. For me, being a freelancer is much more than just a (self-)employment status. It's a state of mind as well as a way of working.

I started freelancing over twenty-five years ago and haven't looked back. I now split my time between producing TV and film – which is where I started out – supporting creative businesses in the West Midlands where I live, and mentoring and teaching other freelancers.

Many of these have come to freelancing as a necessity prompted by a change in their personal circumstances such as redundancy, relocation or a change in family responsibilities. Whatever the reason, going freelance, whilst ultimately rewarding, can be an unsettling and stressful experience.

In this book I will take you through the steps necessary to become a successful freelancer and distil the lessons I've learned over the years. Whilst my experience has largely been in the creative industries – a sector in which the proportion of freelancers is three times the UK national average – I know, from personal experience, that the challenges faced by all freelancers are similar. My aim is to take you on a journey to being the best freelancer you can be, whether you are just embarking on a freelance career or looking to professionalize the way you currently operate.

Freelancing has its own set of skills that can be taught and learned. In many ways it is akin to running a small business. Not only will you be working *in* your business, doing what you do, you will also need to devote time to work *on* your business. Of course, freelancing is not ideal for everyone, but with the world of work changing and freelancers becoming an increasingly significant part of the workforce, it is not unlikely that you will at some point become a freelancer, if not by design then by necessity. Being freelance is not as daunting as it sounds, and it can also be truly liberating.

So, is being a freelancer a career choice or a necessity? In the past it was more often a stopgap between permanent positions than an active career choice. I remember answering the question 'What do you do?' with a slightly apologetic 'I'm a freelancer,' as if freelancing were the preserve of an inferior species not good enough to secure permanent employment. These days it is increasingly common to be a freelancer, particularly in the digital and creative sectors where companies are seeking high-level specialist skills for short-term projects.

Companies now expect to be able to hire in such talent and expertise as required. Freelancers provide them with additional support for busy periods without increasing overheads. Consequently, there are more freelance opportunities than ever and growing numbers of freelancers offering their services.

Freelancing is no longer a stopgap or a personal choice but a necessity if you are to flourish in the modern work environment. This book will show you how.

1.

WHAT DOES BEING FREELANCE MEAN?

In order to understand what is meant by freelancing it is useful to start by looking at how it differs from being employed. The largest single difference between employment and freelancing is accountability. As an employee you are accountable to your boss and the company. As a freelancer you are accountable only to yourself.

If you are an employee, then each month your employer pays your salary into your bank account. The amount you receive includes deductions such as income tax, social security or national insurance, pension contributions, student loans and anything else your employer is entitled or obliged to take. Also, your employer is usually legally obliged to offer paid holiday* and, in the UK, to provide a pension scheme. In return, your employer will stipulate your working hours and your place of work. Your boss will decide what work you do, and the company will be responsible for providing work for you on an ongoing basis.

Contrast this with the freelancing world, where you will be paid

* The United States is the only industrialized nation that does not require employers to offer staff paid leave or public holidays. It shares this distinction with Kiribati, the Marshall Islands, Micronesia, Nauru, Palau and Tonga.

only for the work that you do, and then only after you have submitted a valid invoice in accordance with the client company's terms. Your first commission or assignment will probably be accompanied by a series of forms to fill in – to verify your freelance status and to get yourself set up on their finance system so that they can be in a position to pay you. Then, once you've done the work, you will need to send in your invoice for approval.

Only then will the company be willing to pay you, and this will be in accordance with their payment terms. The good news is that, when you do receive the money, you receive it in full – there are no payroll-type deductions made when you are paid. The bad news is that you have to put some of the money aside to cover your tax bill when it arrives.

As an employee, your employer would usually provide you with whatever you needed to do your work whereas freelancers are expected to provide their own tools of the trade. It's like hiring a plumber to fix a leak: you'd expect them to turn up with everything necessary to sort out your problem. As a freelancer, you are hired to deliver a service and you should have the tools at your disposal to provide that service. You also have a responsibility to keep those tools in good working order and up to date.

In short, employees can focus on doing the work they're assigned whereas freelancers must think about *getting* work as well as *doing* it.

Holiday pay is a complex issue and different industry sectors handle it differently due to their varying requirements for freelancers. When freelancing, the rule of thumb always used to be 'no work no pay'. It's not as cut-and-dried as that these days because there are many instances where freelancers may accrue holiday pay as part of their freelance contracts. How this works will depend on where in the world you are working as well as the sort of freelance work you do.

Pensions are a big challenge when you are a freelancer. Cash flow can be very erratic, which means it can be hard to find a set amount of money to lock away on a regular basis, and on top of this you must research and set up any pension scheme yourself.

Freelance working/ self-employment	Employment
Paid by the job	Steady income
Invoice for services and wait for payment	Salary paid regularly into bank
Submit tax return to pay taxes	Tax etc. deducted at source
No work no pay (usually)	Paid holiday (excluding USA)
Self-funded pension	Company pension scheme
Provide own tools/equipment	Company provides tools/equipment
Flexible hours	Employer determines hours
Flexible schedule	Work as directed
Source your own work	Employer provides work

When you compare the two, the scales appear to be firmly tilted towards employment: why would anyone choose to be a freelancer?

For me, that comparison tells only half the story. What's great about freelancing is that you organize your own time. There are no set hours. You work when you want to or need to. There's nowhere you're expected to turn up every working day. You can legitimately spend your time drinking coffee in your favourite café with your laptop and your mobile. You are the boss – what you say goes. You bang the drum. No one is going to tell you off if you have a lie-in on a quiet day or if you've had a late one the night before. (Remember, though, it's one thing as an employee going into the office and sitting at your desk pretending to work – but when you're the boss, you set the work. It's only yourself you are letting down.)

I relish the freedom of choosing the work I want to do rather than having it dictated to me, despite the difficulty of having to find it myself. (You can wait until it lands on a plate in front of you – but good luck with that strategy.)

For me it's all about the balance between working *in* and *on* your business. By this I mean working *in* your business is doing the work your clients hire and pay you to do. Working *on* your business is doing all the work that supports the running of your freelance career, i.e. handling expenses, chasing unpaid invoices, writing proposals, replying to emails, meeting clients, networking, conferences, training courses and professional development. This all takes time, and some of it can cost you money too. One of the keys to being a successful freelancer is managing this tricky balancing act.

It's not challenging when the workload is low and there is time to work *on* your business. It's much harder in a busy period to take time out from paid work to keep on top of all that other stuff. On the flipside, self-motivation is tough when things are quiet and you're grappling with a tricky task.

If you've recently switched from employment to freelancing then you may be debating whether your working pattern still needs to be nine to five, Monday to Friday. Naturally, you will have to fit in broadly with the hours of your clients, but think about how you can develop a pattern that works for *you*. It can be hard to adjust to this new way of life. You may no longer have a journey to and from work – which sounds fantastic on the surface, but actually that commute could have been when you prepared yourself for the day or wound down. When your office is a desk in your spare room, your working day is completely different from anything you've known before.

Yes, it's a great freedom but there are also changes to get used to and new routines to build. Finding ways to unwind at the end of the day without an obvious change in your location or view can be surprisingly hard. Whereas before you might have had the support and infrastructure of a large organization, now the work all rests on your shoulders. It can be lonely and isolating; you can go a whole day without talking to anyone.

On the flipside, you are in charge of your own destiny. When you are working from your freelance office no one is watching the clock, timing how long or when your breaks are – except you. You can work when you like and where you like. I'll often start early, before most people are in work, and get ahead for the day. Then I might take a longish break mid-morning – nip to the shops, do some chores or have a shower. I'm still putting in the hours I need to; I'm just doing it in a way that allows me to integrate freelance working and family life.

When I am mentoring or running seminars it's at this point where I ask the participants, 'How does this make you feel?' It's a situation I love and relish, but for many it is completely terrifying and seems full of risk.

There are a series of statements that get to the heart of being a freelancer (see figure), designed to determine whether you are freelancing by choice or by necessity and to help you identify the areas you will need to improve on in order to succeed.

Marketplace	**Score 0 – 5**
I am confident in my ability to deliver good work	
There is a culture of freelancing in my area of work	
There are few employed jobs in my area of work	
I have extensive personal networks	
I have a good track record in my area of work	
TOTAL out of 25	

Mindset	**Score 0 – 5**
I value my independence	
I am well organized	
I am self-disciplined	
I enjoy project work	
I am happy to work on my own	
I like meeting new people	
TOTAL out of 30	

Money	**Score 0 – 5**
Irregular income doesn't faze me	
I know my value in the marketplace	
I am not afraid to ask to be paid for my work	
TOTAL out of 15	

For each statement give yourself a score from 0 to 5, 0 indicating that you strongly disagree and 5 indicating that you strongly agree. As you total your score for each section, note how high each total is relative to the possible maximum. If you are scoring less than 50 per cent in any section then that is likely to be an area you will need to work hard on improving.

If your low score is in the area of marketplace then you'll need to focus more on your marketing and engagement with clients, building your networks and appreciating that you may need to sell the freelance opportunity to them alongside your services.

If you're below average in the area of mindset then you'll have to find strategies that give you more security in the work you do and/or more structure to your working day. You'll probably benefit from having at least one major client with whom you can interact face to face and possibly work from their office. If that isn't possible then you might want to find a local co-working space that you can work from and treat like your place of work.

If you score badly in the area of money, you will want to ensure you have a good pitch written and ready to go for clients explaining what benefits you can offer to their business. (You will find more on pitches in Chapter 6, 'Articulating Your Vision', and detail about self-worth in Chapter 5, 'Valuing Yourself'.)

If you are scoring well in each area, that's great news. It sounds like freelancing is going to suit you and the work you do, but don't despair if you have a low score in some or even all areas. Whilst freelancing is something that some people take to very easily, for others it involves a great deal of hard work. A good support network of family and friends is invaluable. It's also a great help if you can connect with other freelancers so you can share knowledge and support each other, particularly when you're finding life difficult.

Be assured that every freelancer finds it tough at times, whatever their level of experience.

WRITING YOUR FREELANCE WORKING AGREEMENT WITH YOURSELF

Chances are, you are going to be working on your own quite a lot with no formal structure to your working day or week. A freelance working agreement with yourself outlines the boundaries within which you are going to work. It's something that you can put together now about how you plan to manage your time and do your work. It's an opportunity for you to reflect on what times of day you work best, how many hours you plan to work a week and how you will slot in your other commitments whilst still doing the hours you are aiming for each week.

You can mould how you want to work to suit you. It has to satisfy your clients' needs as well, but that doesn't necessarily mean sticking to the traditional nine-to-five.

Write a list of things you give yourself permission to do during the working week that will keep you sane and increase your productivity. In my experience, chaining yourself to a desk for eight hours a day without breaks five days a week does not increase productivity. I like to give myself permission to do things during the traditional working week that energize me and make me a better freelancer.

Now it's not to say that I can't do the things that distract me during my working day, not least because I need social media for work. I just need to be aware that these activities can suck me in for extended periods of time and I must be vigilant about this.

I'm not saying you don't need to work hard; I probably work harder as a freelancer than I have in any 'job' I've ever done – but I do it *my* way. Clients I work with will be familiar with the influx of emails from me at 7 a.m. on Sunday morning – it's a time I often use for catching up from the previous week and getting ahead for the next one. This is generally because I'm awake and the rest of the house is sleeping, so I can do this without disturbing the family weekend.

Making work work for you is an important part of your freelance mindset.

Things that help with my work:

- ✓ I am an early bird so starting early and having a proper break mid-morning is OK
- ✓ It is OK to work from home in my pyjamas
- ✓ It is OK to have coffee with friends once or twice a week
- ✓ Going for a walk/run is good thinking time
- ✓ I am more productive after yoga/gym
- ✓ Making a cup of tea and doing the washing at the same time is pure efficiency
- ✓ ....
- ✓ ....
- ✓ ....
- ✓ ....
- ✓ ....

Things that I get distracted by that don't help with work:

- × Social media
- × YouTube
- × Calls or texts from family and friends
- × Household chores
- × ....
- × ....
- × ....
- × ....

FINDING YOUR WORK–LIFE BALANCE

The freelance working agreement with yourself is part of finding your work–life balance. Imagine a set of scales, the old-fashioned sort with two pans. If one side is your work and one side is the rest of your life you are looking for that point of balance where, for you, the two are in kilter with each other and the system is in equilibrium. That point is different for everyone and can shift throughout your career. The key is to understand where yours is right now and to implement systems and strategies to keep it where you want it to be. It's also important, when freelancing, to look at your longer-term work–life balance. You can't control when the work arrives, so you might have a mountain of things to do one month and very little the next. It can be a hard regime to adjust to and it requires you to look further ahead than you might be accustomed to and find new ways to achieve your work–life balance.

I spent the early part of my career in TV production, which is intensive, fast-turnaround project-based work. When I was hired for a production my first action was to book a holiday for the end of the contract. I knew that if I didn't do it straight away, I'd never end up taking the time off. It was my self-preservation mechanism. I knew I was about to work really hard and that holiday was, for me, the light at the end of the tunnel.

These days I work on much shorter projects and tend to be booked by the day or week for a project, rather than months. This means I have to find new ways of instilling that balance away from work. It might be as simple as a day spent pottering around the house when no one else is home, or catching up with friends for a coffee. It's the time I take to recharge my batteries and it is really important.

I can keep up the work façade relatively easily when I'm running on empty but it's not so easy to keep it up at home. That's when I know I need to restore balance. As a freelance working mum, I relate strongly to this quote from Annabel Crabb, an Australian political journalist:

> The obligation for working mothers is a very precise one: the feeling that one ought to work as if one did not have children, while raising one's children as if one did not have a job.

I find that most of the time I can busk my way through and I make this work. This is primarily due to the autonomy that being a freelancer gives me. I can be working anywhere and at any time. Now that is, of course, a double-edged sword – but it's a double-edge I'll accept any day. I can be in the park with the kids and they can be climbing trees. I'll sit on a bench and watch them enjoying their freedom and also be finalizing a meeting or replying to a quick email. So, yes, I'm 'on' all the time but I also have freedom to be working where I want to be and not chained to a desk. That's the work–life balance choice that I've made. A key part of this for me is to be around for the family.

The one thing I do ensure is that I take work at a rate that I'm happy with, and always work hard for my clients to ensure I deliver high-quality results in a user-friendly and timely fashion.

BEING 'SECURE IN INSECURITY'

Most freelancers have work in their diaries for only the next few months, weeks or even days. This is quite usual, a key part of successful freelancing is to be secure in such insecurity. This is easier said than done and can be especially hard if you are more accustomed to traditional employment. It can be very daunting, forever having to pitch your services (rather than doing your job) and never knowing what work is on the horizon.

I use this lack of job security as motivation. It drives me to be constantly chasing the next opportunity and discover the next chunk of work. Even as an experienced freelancer it is eerie when the calendar remains stubbornly blank and there is no confirmed work ahead. I use such occasions to take stock of my network and get out there and catch up with people, remind them I am about and see what might be happening that I can get involved in.

If your need for security is very strong but the work you love is available only on a freelance basis, try to develop longer-term client relationships to bring some stability and security into your working life. If you are someone who has found yourself freelancing by necessity, perhaps following a change in circumstances or a relocation, then you might be better suited to freelance work that more closely resembles employment.

Freelancing is a continuum with, at one end, what might be termed 'extreme' freelancers doing very short contracts for many clients and at the other end those who sell their services for projects of six months' duration or more. Both are freelance, but the latter scenario is much closer to employment than the former and there are likely to be greater expectations from the contracting company and less autonomy for you the further you head along this scale towards quasi-employment.

If you are at the short-contract end of the spectrum and feel too vulnerable, look at developing a broader client offering. Many freelance artists I work with, for example, teach part-time. This brings them more routine and structure as well as a stable income stream.

By understanding where your work naturally sits and where on the freelance continuum you feel comfortable, you can begin to understand the work patterns you are likely to adopt and therefore how to feel secure in them. You might also be able to secure a range of clients that sit in different places along the scale; for example mixing one or two long-term regular clients with several shorter-term ad hoc, varied ones.

FLEXIBILITY

Flexibility is another key attribute for any freelancer. You need to be able to cope with change and be ready to respond. The business landscape is constantly shifting and so are clients' needs. Not to mention that every piece of work is slightly different. As you take on assignments for different clients you will see how the 'same' job can be remarkably different depending on how the client company operates.

In my early days as a production manager working for a series of independent production companies, the same job title and role had widely different expectations depending on the infrastructure of whichever company I was working for. In one, I would be writing cheques weekly for the invoices that needed paying and preparing cost reports for the broadcaster on top of the rest of the work. In another, these responsibilities rested with the accounts department and the head of production, respectively. Being aware of such differences allowed me to target the types of productions and production companies I preferred to work for.

Even longer-term projects demand flexibility. A freelance senior marketing professional might be the only person in their team not in a permanent (staff) position. This in itself can be unsettling, like sitting at the family dinner table while not really being part of the family. Freelancers in this situation are usually contracted for a specific role on a particular project that is well defined, and frequently on a part-time basis. However, the working reality is often quite different. Because they are the only freelancer, they are expected to conform to the workplace norms in that organization; also, as the project evolves and they become more involved with it, extra expectations are placed on them, as if they were a member of staff.

The rest of the team might argue that it's unfair to have a team member who, unlike them, appears to pick and choose what to do. I, however, would argue that the freelancer is fully entitled, since they don't have the same employee benefits or rights and are hired to fulfil a specific brief. It doesn't work both ways.

No freelancer should have to 'take one for the team' if it's not what they've been contracted to do. However, that's sometimes more simply said than done and it's a very easy trap to fall into. Your freelance mindset is saying, 'Please the client, please the client; do what they ask me to do.' But this isn't always the best strategy for the longer-term working relationship.

In the beginning it can all seem to work swimmingly, and you feel you have bedded in well to the project and have become a valuable, even indispensable part of the team. Everything is smelling of roses. But then project creep kicks in. There's a bit more to do. The email volume increases as you are copied in and expected to advise on additional areas. You're expected to be at meetings that are outside your scheduled working hours. Suddenly you're the one working many more hours than contracted. In the beginning you shrug it off. You'll just get through this tricky bit and it'll all be on track again. What's a few extra hours when this client gives you so much work and they are so grateful for what you do?

The reality is that this is likely to become part of a pattern. It won't change. The team you are working with aren't familiar with the details of your engagement. They've probably just been told you are on the team. Why should they treat you any differently? You are all hired to deliver the project. Perhaps the size of the team has grown, and this has affected the dynamics of how everyone is working. Usually none of this is intentional or malicious. (To paraphrase Hanlon's razor: never put down to conspiracy that which can reasonably be attributed to confusion.) And the chances are, this is more misunderstanding than anything else. But this is also where you will need to manage the situation. You don't want to lose your client, but you will if the situation is not managed. (And this client will then turn into one that you *do* want to lose!)

The other side of flexibility is that you have to hit it off straight away with the client and their team and get on with the job. You rarely know anything about each other's lives and what might be going on. It can be a shallow existence, especially when you are new to a client and there is little time or incentive to build friendships.

Contrast this with full-time employment, when you will see the same people day in, day out. You get to know the nitty gritty of each other's lives – the highs and the lows. There is an incentive to find long-term solutions to working harmoniously and dealing with challenging behaviour.

With freelancing there is no such incentive – you simply don't work with that person again. You probably won't even tell them why. It can make for neurotic overachievers. Freelancers worry about whether they are delivering what they are supposed to be delivering so they ensure they do the best job they can and over-achieve in compensation. In the earlier example this is where you need to take control of the situation and bring it to a head before it becomes a real problem, not just for you but for the company you are working with too.

PROFESSIONALISM

You are only as good as your last job, which means that professionalism and reputation are all. You must guard them with your life. The difficulty in the scenario above is that it doesn't mean you should just do everything your client asks. That will lead to you slowly but surely losing that client as you grow more frustrated with project creep and demands that are over and above your agreement and number of hours. It is likely also that the client will become equally frustrated with you since you have been distracted from the original brief and now you aren't delivering what you've been contracted to do.

This is why it is important that you are the grown-up in the conversation and nip such behaviour in the bud before it's too late. Talk to your client about the project, how it's changing, how you think it might get back on track and how you can deliver your part for them.

A senior marketing consultant I mentor found herself in exactly this position. The project had undergone a lot of change in a short period. She was working in a start-up environment that was growing fast; this entailed lots of new hires, which meant the team structure and dynamic were changing. Worse, she was living on another continent from the client and in a different time zone. Project creep set in and as she got dragged further in she became a core part of the operational team and was having to work late into the night owing to the time difference. It wasn't a sustainable situation.

As someone new to freelancing and the breadwinner in her

family, she wasn't sure how to fix the situation, but she knew it wasn't working for her or for them. The growth of the team warranted a full-time, senior, office-based team member. She was beginning to realize that she needed to uncouple herself operationally from the day-to-day (and not be working all night) and refocus her role with the organization as a more executive, strategic consultant rather than an operational one. Splitting the workload in this manner would mean a smaller, less lucrative contract, of course, but it was the right thing for both the project and the company, and hence the professional thing to do.

Professionalism is more than how you behave in any single situation, though. It must permeate every aspect of the way you operate. Every experience your client has with you needs to be professionally conducted. Think about when you visit a high-end department store. You expect the staff to be able to assist you and be knowledgeable about the items you are interested in. A good store will be certain to make sure it is the right purchase for you. They value their long-term relationship with you. They will never sell you something unsuitable simply because they can. Now consider how you can deliver this type of professional high-end service for all your clients.

Professionalism should be at the forefront of your mind in all the work you do. The entire 'user-journey' your clients navigate whilst working with you should be professional, from the email address you use to the timely fashion and manner with which you respond to clients, and how you handle payments. By ensuring every step is professional you will build and maintain a strong reputation with your clients.

SELF-DISCIPLINE

Good freelancers are disciplined people. They get to meetings on time, they are reliable. They communicate in a timely fashion with their clients. They know if they have the capacity to take on more work or if they need to recommend a colleague. Freelancing is a marathon, not a sprint, so keeping your house in order will serve you well in the long term.

If you aren't by nature the most disciplined person you will need to work hard at this to ensure that you keep abreast of everything you need to do. Equally, even the most self-disciplined people can be guilty of putting off the least interesting jobs.

REPUTATION

You are delivering your own service to your clients. There's no one and no company to hide behind; the buck stops with you. And this is where your reputation comes in. It's your currency. You want to be seen to be the person who delivers, delivers well and does so with a smile on their face.

Your reputation needs to be valued and nurtured. It invariably arrives before you do, in the form of recommendations from clients and colleagues, so you want to make sure it is a good one and the sort that the clients you want to work with will value. There's more detail on values in the next chapter, but it's important to realize that you can have what looks like on the surface a good reputation but, in reality, is one that is not valued by your potential clients.

An example of this might be that you are known for detailed work that is very intricate and takes considerable time to deliver. On the surface, this sound likes a good reputation to have, but it might be that your potential clients don't need that level of detail for their work. They might consider, based on your reputation, that you would take too long or be too expensive for the work they need doing.

Letting down your clients can have long-term consequences for your reputation. They will vote with their feet. They aren't your employer; they don't have to give you a reason to move on to another freelancer to deliver the work for them. It's tough, but you really can't afford an off day. You are expected to be on top form for every hour your client is paying you. Let a client down and the word will spread.

You want to be the person with a strong reputation that other people recommend because you are so good at what you do.

FEAST AND FAMINE

Feast and famine are both big issues for freelancers. When you are in famine you have to find ways to 'cope' and during the feast period you have to find ways to manage the workload. It's easy to focus on the famine side of freelancing and how you need to develop skills to deal with, and enjoy, the quiet times whilst also looking for new work. What is less often thought about are the challenges associated with feast.

Lack of work can be very worrying and stressful. Your brain will tell you you'll never get work again. But so long as you are good at what you do, and you have a wide network and leverage it, that is nonsense. Take a step back and look at the wider context of your working environment. Think about what time of year it is – if it's July or December then you're probably better off taking a break. New projects don't tend to start then as companies are entering holiday season, projects are often coming to an end and new ones will kick off in January or September. If you have a good relationship with your clients they might drop you a line and say that there is work coming up after the holidays. Give yourself a break and take some time off too.

If you don't think your famine is seasonally related, and particularly if you've been a freelancer for a few years, have a look back at your old diaries and see whether these were quiet times also. The 'famine' might just be cyclical. In some companies the last couple of months of their financial year can mean a spurt of spending and commissioning freelance projects, in others it's a time when the budgets are all spent and people close off their projects and get ready for the new budgets in the new financial year, when their spending will start again.

The likelihood is that the reason you are in famine is less to do with you and more to do with circumstance. So, take the pressure off yourself and allow some time to regroup and think about what comes next. It's likely there are potential clients out there you would love to work with, but you haven't had the chance to develop a relationship with them. Famine is the time to make that approach and connect with them.

If you are new to freelancing, then at the start it can feel as though the work will never come in; worrying about feast times seems impossible. And having 'too much work' does sound good. In theory. They can't get enough of you. Marvellous, that's what you'd been working hard for. Until you think about the reality of more work than you can comfortably handle all landing at once. The reality is that it's incredibly tough. Especially if it all comes from different but important clients. It can be hard, almost impossible, to turn any of it down and unfeasible to delay it. If it has all been offered by important clients, you'll need to think hard about what you can really take on. How many extra hours a day can you put in and for how long? If it's a couple of weeks or a month you might just about be able to keep all the balls in the air, but any longer and you'll struggle to keep going.

Before you take on work when you are in feast, take a moment to consider whether you can deliver it to the standard you'd like for the client before you accept the work. Be realistic about your capacity. The client would rather know now that you are too busy than have it cancelled further down the line because you can't manage it.

Just as you should take a step back when faced with famine, you should do the same in feast and put it in context. A common explanation for feast is that you are undercharging for your services. It's easy to do, especially if you've not had much work recently: you lose confidence, offer potential clients a lower price than usual to tide you over and then they all want your services. Bingo! You are in feast, but you are being a busy fool, working too hard and not being properly recompensed for your work. There's more on how to value yourself and your time in Chapter 5, 'Valuing Yourself'.

The key is to be honest with your clients at all times and manage their expectations. If you say you can take on the work, that has to mean you can do it to your usual standard. If you can't, then you need to think carefully about what you can realistically deliver for them and whether it will be good enough. It's your reputation, after all.

SELF-MOTIVATION

Self-motivation is what makes good freelancers stand out from the crowd. You can be the best at what you do, but if you aren't self-motivated then you will struggle with being a freelancer and getting work in the quiet times. There's always more you can be doing. Self-motivation is about doing that bit more. It's about working *on* your business as well as *in* your business.

To be a successful and sustainable freelancer it's not enough to wait for the phone to ring or the emails to land asking you to do some work. You've got to be out there getting in front of people and looking for work both online and offline, finding and nurturing opportunities and clients.

Think about whether this is something you will struggle with. If so, devise some strategies to keep yourself going at such times. There's more on how you do this in Chapter 8, 'Nurturing and Leveraging Your Network'.

EMOTIONAL INTELLIGENCE

Emotional intelligence is the ability to manage not only your emotions but also those of the people around you. It's about knowing how you are feeling and the impact this has on those around you. You want to be the grown-up and not the stroppy teenager. Be the diplomat, read the client and keep them informed. Work out how they like to be kept up to date. Be honest with the client about what you can and can't do. It's OK not to be able to do things – you aren't hired to be able to do everything – but be curious and keen to learn.

Be reliable and visible when you are working for them. Some clients like a set day or hours, others are more flexible. Find that out from the start and play by that client's rules. That doesn't mean they've hired you to say yes to everything they ask you to do. They've hired you for your expertise, so it's OK to push back, but be personable about it. It's amazing how far a sense of humour can take you with a client.

SWITCHING ON AND SWITCHING OFF

Switching on and switching off can be very different when you're accountable only to yourself.

I've known freelancers to go for a walk round the block before they start work and at the end of each day, as if mimicking a journey to and from a place of work will allow them time to prepare for the day mentally and switch off at the end of it.

If much of your work is done from home, then you may have days or even weeks when you rarely step outside. Making yourself a work zone within your home into which you go to work and then step out of at the end of the day can provide you with a structure and strategy to switch on and off. And be strict with yourself that when you leave it, you leave your work behind. It doesn't mean you have to work nine to five. You can work the hours that best suit you. It's just important that you recognize the difference between being at work and at home and allowing yourself time off to relax and unwind. You'll do a better job when you are working if you can unwind and switch off regularly.

The same is true of your mobile phone. It can be your best friend, allowing you to respond to that urgent query when in fact you're walking the dog mid-morning. However, it's also hard to not get ruled by your phone and its regular buzzing in your pocket all day and evening. I know it's easier said than done, but it's good to take a break from it. Not everything has to be answered within five minutes of landing on your desk.

Whilst it's true that when you are on the job you *do* need to be on top of your game, you also need to find strategies to enable you to switch off. If you allow yourself to be constantly on you will burn out and become less productive. It's important you set your own ground rules and boundaries from the start. That's not to say that you can't break them from time to time during busy periods, but recognize that's what you are doing and make sure you readjust again afterwards.

THE SUCCESSFUL FREELANCE PSYCHE

The successful freelance psyche is much like a stool. It's only functional when the three legs are bearing equal weight.

The three legs represent the three key qualities of a freelancer: **desires** (♥), **skills** (♦) and **finances** (£). Successful freelancers are those who are focussed **equally** on each quality and sit comfortably atop the stool and keep it in balance.

Think about what happens if you take away one of the three legs.

- Remove finances and you are left with desires and skills, but that's a hobby. A hobby isn't going to feed or clothe you.
- Desires and finances alone are all style over substance and you are going to struggle to build a sustainable freelance career in the long term.
- With only skills and finances you are going to struggle to tell the world you are out there.

All in all, to be a successful freelancer you need to think about your abilities in these three areas and how you can develop all three so that they complement and support each other and remain in balance.

THE FREELANCE TRAP

Even the most hardened freelancers find themselves looking at job adverts and applying for them. Every freelancer I've worked with has been guilty of this – myself included.

Each time I think, *It'll be different this time. I've matured.* (That old chestnut – it's never going to happen.) *This company is different, I will be able to hack it.*

This is particularly true in the famine times when work is quieter and I'm trying to find new clients and new projects. I come upon job adverts – *Maybe I should go for one of these*, I think. *I have the skills to do this*, I think. *Then I won't have to look for new clients and people will even pay me to go on holiday*, I think.

By this stage I have forgotten my horror of office politics and the systems and that yes, *they will expect me in all day, every day and that does include school holidays – all of them*. And even though the daily rate may be much less than my freelance rate – I'll still end up better off by the end of the year . . .

THAT'S BECAUSE I'M EXPECTED TO WORK ALL DAY, EVERY DAY.

Don't get me wrong. I do work, and I work hard both *on* and *in* my business. But I do it my way. I can't say I always do it when I want to do it, but I do make sure I balance my work and home life and that I can do the school runs more than just occasionally. And I am around during the school holidays. Because these things are important to me.

And every time I dip my toe in the water of employment, I last a *maximum* of five months before the inevitable implosion. Inevitable is my husband's word – he doesn't say it at the time as I'm always super-excited and convinced I can do it this time and he's hugely supportive – but when it's all over and I look back, he says, 'Well that was inevitable wasn't it? You're not made to be an employee.' He can see from the start that the writing is on the wall.

These days, being freelance is not a synonym for unemployed or between jobs. It's a badge to wear with pride, whether you are freelance by necessity or design. It usually takes a good six months to go from zero to hero, but it won't happen for you if you are just biding your time waiting for a permanent position to come up. You need to commit to freelancing and work at it.

Now you understand what being freelance is all about. It's time to get started on finding your own freelance identity.

2.

FINDING YOUR FREELANCE IDENTITY

How you feel about the job you do and the balance between your life and your work is extremely important. Only by recognizing your boundaries and taking time to know and understand yourself will you be able to plan your freelance career to be as stimulating and rewarding as you would wish.

When I work with freelancers in my workshops, I use three main tools to unlock this internal conversation: personality tests; the distinction between 'I' and 'T'-shaped people and, finally, a skills audit.

PERSONALITY TESTS

Whilst I don't subscribe to the view that personality tests are some kind of silver bullet, I do think they can add value and insight to your self-awareness. They give you a snapshot of your current situation and reflect back to you how you are thinking as you take the test. In my view, one of the more useful personality tests of the many that are available is the work done by Edgar H. Schein on career anchors. Schein identifies eight such anchors that indicate your values, needs and competencies. The eight anchors work on a sliding scale, so for each one you can decide if you identify very strongly for or against, or if you find yourself somewhere in the middle. Three are talent based, three needs based and two values based.

Of the eight anchors, the three that are most relevant to freelancers are:

- **THE ENTREPRENEURIAL CREATIVITY ANCHOR**
  Scoring highly here indicates you want to build your own enterprise and that you measure your success by doing so.
- **THE SECURITY/STABILITY ANCHOR**
  A low score here indicates you are comfortable in insecurity and will be less likely to struggle emotionally with being a freelancer.
- **THE AUTONOMY/INDEPENDENCE ANCHOR**
  A high scorer here does not easily give up the opportunity to define their own work in their own way and will often opt to be a freelancer doing highly autonomous work.

These anchors highlight well the mindset of a successful freelancer. For me, what is great about Schein's method is that there are no right or wrong answers. It just describes who you are and how you see the world. Once you are armed with this knowledge you can target the work that will suit you best and build your freelance career based on who you are and what you were born to do. It's about what makes you tick and being comfortable in your skin. The more insight you can gain into yourself, the more likely you are to succeed as a freelancer.*

* If you would like to undertake an in-depth assessment, the full career anchors questionnaire is available to purchase online at https://www.careeranchorsonline.com/.

'I' AND 'T'-SHAPED PEOPLE

The second tool I use to help unlock freelance identities is the 'I'- and 'T'-shaped people analysis. Traditional freelancing has in the main been pursued by people who are technical specialists, hired for their expertise. You could call them 'I'-shaped people as their work requires great depth of experience in one technical area but little breadth of knowledge in any other. These freelancers – photographers, graphic designers and architects are all examples – will deliver the same service to each client they work for.

If the height of your 'I' represents your experience then, in the beginning, your 'I' will be pretty short, and it can be a Catch 22 situation trying to find work: you don't have the experience so you don't get the job, but if you don't get the job then you can't acquire experience. In a world of 'I'-shaped people it can be hard to gain traction at the start of your career.

Fortunately, these 'I'-shaped areas often require the support of less-specialist personnel such as assistant roles that provide the training ground for you to gain experience. Alternatively, new-entrant 'I'-shaped freelancers may start to build their professional portfolios working for smaller clients with limited budgets.

With every piece of work you do your 'I' gets longer as your depth of experience increases. The big challenge in any 'I'-shaped role is making the step change from one level up to the next, and finding the right opportunity to do so. It can involve leaving your comfort zone and taking on new challenges, and it can also mean breaking away from a client or group of people you've worked with regularly. This can be both challenging and exciting.

Whilst 'I'-shaped freelancing work does still exist, there is also a growing area that requires a different type of thinking and a different skillset. These roles are more managerial – not something you'd automatically associate with being a freelancer. A good example is the role of a film or TV producer. A producer needs to be able to solve complex problems, and they are hired to do just that. Then they bring in and manage the highly technically competent people (the 'I's) to realize the film for them.

Such people have not only depth of experience (the 'I') but also the ability to collaborate with others right across their sector, making them 'T'-shaped.

If you are an 'I'-shaped person, clients hire you because you have the knowledge and experience to do something specific. You solve technical problems or provide an expert service. If you are a 'T'-shaped person, it can be harder for clients to identify where you sit and what expertise you bring to the table – it can appear at times that you are jack of all trades and master of none. It's only when you realize the value of being the translator, the enabler, the collaborator that you begin to understand how much value the 'T'-shaped person can add.

As a TV production manager, I was trained to adopt a 'T'-shaped mindset very early on. I needed to be knowledgeable in all aspects of production management – logistics, budgeting, health and safety, insurance etc. – and I also needed to be able to communicate this at a professional and knowledgeable level with all the production team and crew involved in the production.

I didn't need to know how to operate a camera to talk to a camera operator, but I did need to know what sort of camera they might want to use for this production and why. I had to do the same with the sound engineers, the art department, post production and so on. They were all the experts – the 'I'-shaped people; I was the enabler, and part of my role was to identify where an issue in one area would have an impact on another. I had to have the breadth of vision to make the whole project come together logistically.

Another thing to remember about 'T'-shaped people is that everyone's 'T' is a slightly different shape. Some are wide and skinny, and some are short and fat. There is no right or wrong about this, but you do need an awareness of what shape you are and, just like a game of Tetris, you need to see where your 'T' fits so you can find work that plays to your strengths.

When you are reflecting on yourself and your skills it is useful to look at the work you do and enjoy and identify whether you are an 'I' or a 'T' shape.

Draw your 'I' or 'T' here to reflect your work and experience:

SKILLS AUDIT

The final tool I use regularly to help my clients understand more about themselves is the skills audit. This is a simple tool that asks you to take a snapshot of the skills you have now, then to look ahead to where you want to be, and the skills and experience that will be required to get you there. In this way you can create an action plan for acquiring or improving the requisite skills to reach your goal.

It's based on the principle that if you want to do better work, you need to focus on your weaker areas more than your stronger areas. This is not easy; human nature makes us want to get better at things we are already good at. These also tend to be the areas you like the best. To improve the not so good you have to take the comfortable coat off and put in the hard yards.

Irrespective of your level, you need to know what your skills are. The skills audit is designed to help you identify these and generate a plan to work on. It starts by identifying three types of skill (or expertise) – hard, soft and other.

Hard skills are specific to the industry you work in and – by definition – less transferable to other fields.

Soft skills are the universal personal and interpersonal tools that are easily transferable across industries. Examples include communications skills, IT, leadership, problem solving, working with and relating to others, and applying initiative.

Other skills are any skills, knowledge or expertise you possess that don't fit easily into one of the other two categories. They could be from previous work you have done in an unrelated field, a hobby or the languages you speak.

Your skills can then be audited in the following five-step process:

STEP 1 – WHERE AM I NOW?

Using the table on page 33, write a bullet-point list of your knowledge and skills that are important for the work you do currently (or have done most recently). Aim to identify about fifteen bullet points and then mark each as either hard, soft or other.

STEP 2 – WHERE DO I WANT TO BE?

The first part of this step is to visualize what your future work would be – say in three to five years' time. Write it down. Next write a list of the knowledge and skills important for this future scenario. You should again have about fifteen bullet points, and again mark each as either hard, soft or other.

STEP 3 – HOW GOOD AM I?

The next step is to rate your ability against each bullet point, on both lists using the following five-point scale.

- **0** No ability
- **1** A tiny bit
- **2** OK
- **3** Good
- **4** Expert

Go through each skill you have noted down and rate each point individually across both steps 1 and 2.

STEP 4 – CORROBORATION

Now find someone who knows you well and whose opinion you trust to review what you've written and, without looking at your ratings, to rate your abilities using the same scoring system. Choose someone who will be honest with you, will challenge you and who understands the work you do. This allows you to corroborate your self-perception with how someone else sees you. Unsurprisingly, the two can be quite different. Often, the things you take for granted in yourself are what others value most.

Where am I now? ....

Current Skills and Knowledge	Hard / Soft /Other	My Rating 0 – 4	Peer Rating 0 – 4	Discrepancy

Where do I want to get to? ....

Future Skills and Knowledge	Hard / Soft /Other	My Rating 0 – 4	Peer Rating 0 – 4	Discrepancy

STEP 5 – APPLICATION

Now review what you have written and what your reviewers have said and look at areas where there are discrepancies. These will be areas where you think you can or can't do something and your reviewers think the reverse. These are the interesting areas where you don't know yourself so well, so it is worth taking time to look at these skills in detail and think about what you can learn. You might want to go back to your reviewer(s) and discuss the discrepancies with them.

Now, using the table opposite, put together an action plan detailing

1. The skills you want to improve and the skills you need to gain – a good place to start is by concentrating on developing the lower-scoring areas.
2. Which skills will it be most beneficial to improve first – remember to be realistic about how much time this will take since you've still got to earn your living. Prioritize current skills over future ones.
3. What skills you can develop within the work you are already doing – perhaps there are short courses available that you can take, or a regular client who might allow you to get involved in new areas that could be of mutual benefit.
4. Rate the urgency of the improvement and allocate a deadline to achieve it by.

This is now your action plan for developing your skills and enhancing your offering to current and future clients. It is up to you to ensure you meet your deadlines and have the skills you need to do the work you do. It's harder than it sounds: you will have to take time out from paid work to do this.

The skills audit can be used periodically to assess how well you are developing your career and to identify new skills gaps that may occur as you build experience and look to grow further. If you find

Action Plan

Skills to improve	Current / future	Course / on the job	Urgency: hi / med / low	Deadline

that you have a quite disparate set of skills or experiences, you might be more suited to a portfolio career.

PORTFOLIO CAREERS

If your answer to the question 'What do I do?' contains three or more answers that seem not to have any logical connection, then you probably have a portfolio career.

For me this is a very specific type of freelancing. A photographer might consider that working on film sets, at weddings and as a photography teacher comprises a portfolio career. I disagree, because each element requires the same *technical expertise* and their skill as a photographer is merely being implemented across a range of customer segments (more about segments later) to balance out their time and income.

A *true* portfolio career means being hired by different clients for your *different areas of technical expertise* rather than for your ability to use the *same technical expertise in different situations*.

Mine is a portfolio career. I might be booked as a line producer for outside broadcasts by production companies, as a trainer and mentor by universities for employability and enterprise programmes, or as a strategic consultant by screen sector organizations and creative businesses. I am able to offer this portfolio of very specific yet quite diverse services to potential clients owing to the experience gained and skills I have built up over the years.

I like having a portfolio of services to offer, but I have to admit to having a very low boredom threshold, so the constant variety and the different challenges keep me stimulated. This approach doesn't suit everyone, of course, and there's no great career benefit to offering a portfolio of services to potential clients; if anything it's harder, as you have a whole range of skills to offer and therefore a wider client base to keep happy. You'll see in Chapter 3, 'The 3 Rs: Research, Research, Research', that for each service you offer you are going to need to do distinct market research – which means a lot more work.

At this stage it's more about *looking inside yourself* as you find your freelance identity, *reflecting* on the work you do, or plan to do, and *understanding* whether you want or need to offer a portfolio of services.

WHAT DOES SUCCESS MEAN TO ME?

Success is about attaining what *you* set out to achieve. It is a completely subjective measurement. It's not about comparing yourself with others and deeming yourself less successful because you haven't done what they've done. You don't know what they are trying to achieve and what compromises they have made along the way to get to where they are. Comparison is likely to just make you feel like a failure.

If you can define what success means to you then you can set out a plan to achieve it. For a long time I equated success with status and earnings and deemed myself inferior to those who had them. These days, when I consider what success means to me, I realize it is being with my family and doing work I enjoy and find challenging. It's about being able to manage my work so I can be there during the special moments for my kids.

Take a minute to write down what success means to you.

What does success mean to me?

Success stories abound when you look at them through the correct lens. Now that you've thought about this, remember to refer back to what you've written and congratulate yourself when you achieve one of your goals.

PRACTICAL CONSIDERATIONS

The self-examination you've conducted so far to find your freelance identity will give you a good theoretical base from which to start planning your offering. However, real life can often get in the way of the best theories so it is worth considering now what practical considerations you must add to the mix. Here are three of the more common ones:

Geographical If you've relocated from the city to a smaller town you might find that employment opportunities with local companies are a little thin on the ground, so freelancing has become a necessity. In this situation you may find that you need to maintain your longer-distance client relationships and look at how you can re-engineer them to allow you to work remotely whilst working hard to build up local networks and opportunities.

Temporal You might be limited by the number of hours you can commit to working each week. If you have caring responsibilities, for example, freelancing might allow you to do the work you love within the hours you have available.

Circumstantial Perhaps a change in your personal life has forced you to re-evaluate your work and finding or holding down an employed position is no longer an option. Or it could be as straightforward as wanting to reduce the stress in your life and spend more time with your family.

Many freelancers I've worked with have traded in the big corporate job and the many hours of commuting for their hometown and freelancing – and find a release of pressure as they uncouple from corporate life. Whatever the realities of your situation, it's important to be honest with yourself from the start so you can build this into your freelancer planning.

FROM 'REFLECTION' TO PRESENTATION

Now that you've looked inside yourself and begun to discover what your own personal freelance identity is and what skills you have to offer, you can look at how you present yourself to the outside world – your own personal brand. As a consumer you are experienced at responding to brands, but thinking about building your own can be a lot harder.

Even highly experienced marketing directors I've worked with find the idea of selling themselves incredibly tough. Give them a product or a service and they're away, but the thought of selling *themselves* is often completely alien. So don't worry if you are finding this introspection tough. It is, but I can assure you that the harder you work at it and the more in depth you go, the greater will be the rewards as you launch yourself on the market. So, before you start on building your own brand let's look at what you already know about brands.

BRANDS

Brands are everywhere. We all have opinions about them – from supermarkets to fashion to technology. You know what brands you like and don't like. You know which brands you trust and which you don't. You know which brands make you feel good about yourself. You will have opinions on them that go further than any function they fulfil in your life. Even 'no brand' is a brand preference.

When you go into a shop, you know which brands you want to shop for. When you watch television, you know when someone is selling to you in an advert.

To explore how you think about brands more deeply, complete the statements in the box about brands that you interact with every day as a consumer.

My favourite brands are . . . .

Because . . . .

They make me feel . . . .

The brands I trust are . . . .

Because . . . .

They make me feel . . . .

I would pay extra for . . . .

Because . . . .

They make me feel . . . .

My least favourite brands are . . . .

Because . . . .

They make me feel . . . .

The brands I don't trust are . . . .

Because . . . .

They make me feel . . . .

The feelings and descriptions you have written down are the values you associate with each brand. All of us have strong feelings about brands. You can love brands and you can hate them and your feelings for them can change over time. These feelings form part of the whole brand experience along with the logo, the product (or service) and the customer experience. The values *you* associate with a brand may be in line with how the brand wishes to be seen – or they may not. A successful brand ensures its customers' perceptions and experiences align with those of the brand through their entire customer journey.

Now think about the *monetary value* of a brand. You have to pay for the goods or services you want – but consider whether a brand *on its own* can have a monetary value. Think about your shopping preferences – do you pay extra for branded items? Think about your trip around the supermarket: do you mainly purchase branded items? Is your shopping trolley filled with brand leaders such as Heinz tomato ketchup and Tropicana orange juice or do you look for the supermarket own-label products? Think about why you may be willing to pay more for these. I would argue it's because of the brand and the values it espouses of quality and taste.

It's worth noting that logos are not brands. Logos are visual cues – they are how you recognize brands. Brands have values, logos do not. If you decide to create a logo for your services, make sure that it fits well with your brand values and potential customers.

If you are in a creative sector your visual representation is likely to be an important aspect of how your customers perceive you, so creating your brand – and your logo – is likely to add value to your offering.

BUILDING 'BRAND ME'

Building 'Brand Me' is a way of understanding and unlocking what is important to you as a person, what your *values* are. You are selling yourself and your services. They are intertwined: you being you makes you good at the work you do. Your values are unique. They tell you what is important to you and are a reflection of how you want people to see you. They change over time because so do you. It is your values that you show to your prospective clients. The trouble is that few of us are used to articulating our own values or even really thinking about them.

The previous brand exercise helped you understand how you

The value words that resonate for me are . . .

Values that I admire in other brands

Values that are important to me

BRAND ME

Values that I believe a professional freelancer should adopt think and feel about existing brands. Now it is time to turn the spotlight on yourself, examine yourself and identify the brand values that apply to you as a freelance professional. Take some time to consider the *values that are important to you personally* and that *portray how you want the people you work with to see you*.

Have a look back at your notes about brands and look at the words you used to describe your favourite brands and how you feel about them. The good news is that, since you've written about brands that you like, the chances are they will share some of your values – so you've already done some of the heavy lifting. Now all you need to do is look through and find the words that most resonate with you and are most important to you. What other value words are important to you in the work you do? Write down in the box on page 42 as many as you can.

Then review what you've written and pick out six that most represent you and the work you do; this is your brand – Brand Me. These words must encompass your entire offering. Think carefully about the words you choose and avoid platitudes such as 'quality' or 'service'. Write your six words in the 'Brand Me' figure overleaf.

These six words represent the core values of your brand. They underpin how you present yourself to the world.

Take them. Own them. Wear them with pride.

Use them to talk about who you are and what you do.

Interrogate them. Take each value word and write a paragraph about what it means to you and what you do. When you are working and talking to potential clients you need to be able to express and share your values with them. The more words you have up your sleeve to describe your values and what you do, the easier it is to communicate with your clients in ways that they can understand.

Your values give very strong signals to others about who you are and what you stand for. It's much easier to work with those who have similar values to you than with those who have very different ones.

Think about what would happen if you worked with clients who held values starkly different from your own. It's like when dating

misfires – you're not a match. However hard you try both of you will be disappointed by trying to work together and *that won't change*. Move on and find a client who shares your values.

WHAT DO I DO?

Now that you've examined your freelance identity in depth it's time to pull it all together and start to articulate precisely what it is you're offering potential customers in practical terms by answering the question 'What do I do?'

There are actually two parts to this; *what you can offer* is the first part, the second is identifying *why potential customers should choose you*. That comes later: right now you need a concise answer to the first question.

Look back at your skills audit and the 'I'- and 'T'-shaped analysis. Think about what you can ascertain about the skills and experience you can offer. Think about all the things that you can or want to do and write them down.

Write down *all* the skills and experiences that you believe you

THIS IS WHAT I DO . . .

have to offer: start by writing down a stream of consciousness to capture all your thoughts and ideas. Don't worry about organizing them yet, but be sure to take some time over this. It's not an easy task and your brain will try to divert you. Stick with it: you will get past your brain trying to distract you and start to express all the skills and experiences you can offer.

Once you've done this, use a different coloured pen to take a bird's-eye view of what you've written. Look especially for patterns.

- Can you group your information together under one banner that represents a core set of experiences? It doesn't matter if you are 'I'-shaped or 'T'-shaped for this – it's about understanding what you can offer and how your experience and skills join up.
- If you are finding that some of your skills and experiences seem distinct and disparate you might be more suited to a portfolio career.
- Consider whether you have one strand of your portfolio that overshadows the others and is your strongest offering. If that is the case, then focus on this in the first instance.
- If, on the other hand, you have a broad spread and no particular strand is significantly stronger than the others, then you likely do have a portfolio offering and will need to work accordingly.

Now you've worked out your freelance identity, your values and what you can offer, it's time to think about who might be buying. You start this with research.

3.

THE 3 Rs: RESEARCH, RESEARCH, RESEARCH

Making potential customers want to choose you and what you offer is always going to be an uphill struggle if you don't understand their wants and needs. It's not just about understanding the marketplace in which you want to operate – essential though that is – it's about *client-focussed thinking* and answering the question 'Why choose me?'

Marketing is at the core of any successful business enterprise. Master the basics and you will gain clients more quickly and retain them for longer. I can only give you a framework; you need to add your own insights and intuition to make your customers choose you and what you do.

MARKET RESEARCH

Market research can be an expensive and time-consuming activity – large companies spend fortunes on gathering information about their potential customers in order to target them more effectively. Believe it or not, you have some big advantages over these large companies. You are in a niche market. And as an expert in your field you are likely to have a good understanding of your customers' needs and how your services can provide value to them.

Market research tells you who your customers are and which of your services you can sell them. You need it because without this bigger picture you can't make informed decisions about where you fit in and how to market your services.

Remember, you are not the centre of your work, *your customers are*.

The ultimate aim of all this is to achieve sales. Whilst market research and marketing plans can seem like rather formal and scary-sounding concepts, they are just frameworks to provide you with the tools you need to do your own research and write your own plan. It will take a bit of time, but you will reap the rewards later as you bring on new clients. To be effective, marketing activity needs to be structured, not random, and you need to own and take charge of the process.

3Cs ANALYSIS

The first part of your market research is the 3Cs analysis. This helps you determine the basic factors that will enable you to fulfil customers' needs and differentiate yourself from your competition. The 3Cs are:

1. **Company** – This is the 'internal' part that you've already done a lot of work on: What are you good at? Who are you and where do you want to be? What do you do?
2. **Customers** – Who are they? What do they need? Where are they?
3. **Competition** – Who are they and what are they offering (and not offering)? Understanding your competition helps you differentiate yourself and see where you can fit into the ecosystem.

So, 1 is internal, 2 and 3 are external. This framework helps you to understand and define what you offer, how you offer it and what your unique selling proposition (USP) is that will connect with your target market. The 3Cs are the foundation of your market research, which in turn underpins your marketing plan.

You should also be aware that the 3Cs are dynamic – they change over time – and are interdependent: if one changes, one or both of the others do too. You also operate in an evolving and ever-changing marketplace where customers and competitors come and go.

Before drilling down into the 3Cs in detail, remember that if you are a portfolio freelancer then your 3Cs analysis will be different for each strand of the portfolio and you will need to analyse each separately.

COMPANY

In traditional marketing this is an exercise about looking at the entire company you are working in and analysing it. This in effect means that you need to look at yourself as if you were a company and analyse both you and how you are operating. You need to be honest and objective and look at the positives and negatives of what you are doing and how you are operating.

The important thing with this analysis is to look inside, outside and around your work and think about how it interacts with the wider economic and political picture. You also want to think ahead to what your operations might look like in the future.

The framework used here is the SWOT analysis: Strengths, Weaknesses, Opportunities, Threats.

As you conduct your analysis, remember that you want to investigate the good and the not so good about your services. Which will get you more customers: improving the good or improving the not so good? To my mind that's the easy one – improve the not so good. But I know that's easier said than done. The bits you are good at tend to be the bits you enjoy the most and because you like to work on them, you become better and better at them. Like choosing a comfortable old coat to wear, you stick at working on the familiar areas and not devoting time to improving those areas you feel less comfortable in.

Use the box provided as an outline framework for your own analysis.

First investigate your strengths and weaknesses – these are about looking inside your freelance operations and seeing what is working well and what is not. Next, look at the opportunities for getting work, and threats to the work you do, in the environment in which you operate.

The **strengths** of your freelance operation rest in your resources and your capabilities. So, in the strengths box, write down all the aspects of your operations that you regard positively. What are all the things you pride yourself on doing well? What areas do you have expertise in?

Some years ago I decided to get a motorcycle licence. And I wanted a proper motorbike, not a scooter. The experience was dreadful. Not the riding part, that was easy. It was the assumption that I needed a small bike without gears because I was 'a girl' and therefore ill equipped to master 'proper' motorcycles. And trying to get leathers that looked good as well as providing protection? Forget about it.

So I started a business called Girls Angels – a niche motorcycle training school aimed principally at women. I defined the strengths of the company as 'tailored training', 'customer-focussed', 'making motorbiking accessible', and 'high prices'.

These days as a freelance trainer and facilitator I define my strengths as being someone who gets things done, is reliable and offers high-quality training on a range of topics delivered well and with passion. People are buying into me and what I do. Unlike running a company, I can't substitute myself as my clients are buying *me*. A key part of my strengths is me and who I am. Never lose sight of the fact that *you* are a key strength in your freelance offering.

So, when thinking about your strengths, concentrate on what it is about *you* and *your offering* that people are buying in to. What do

My SWOT analysis

Strengths	Weaknesses
Opportunities	**Threats**

you have a good reputation for? If you are not sure, ask people close to you: friends, peers and even possibly those clients with whom you have a good relationship. The things you take for granted about yourself and don't value or acknowledge are the very things that set you apart from others and are your true strengths.

When I talk to students at university who are all studying the same course and looking for quite similar work on graduation, they really struggle to differentiate themselves from each other – all they can see is that they are doing the same course. But then the conversation turns to their hobbies and interests, what other areas of expertise they have, and suddenly the light bulbs start coming on as they realize that they can use these in combination with their education to give each a distinct proposition and build their personal brand.

In the same way that your strengths are personal to you and your freelance offering, so are your **weaknesses**. It is important to be frank with yourself about any weaknesses in your offering. If you can't own up to them then you can't improve.

Additionally, one person's weakness can be another person's strength. For example, a new magazine might hire a launch editor for the first edition, and they then hand over to someone else for Issue 2 onwards. The launch editor's strengths could equally be counted as weaknesses once the magazine is up and running.

Think about the weaknesses in your offering. First, consider if there are areas or aspects where you have an inherent disadvantage – some aspect you are less able to deliver well than another. This could be in terms of the equipment you use to carry out a certain process, or perhaps you are just starting out and you don't have quite the same level of experience as your competitors. It could be as simple as geography – you can't offer an on-call service because you live too far away.

Your resources are an ongoing challenge. You are marketing your services and you can only be doing one thing at a time. Where are you finding that your resources are stretched? Perhaps there are areas of your work that always get left behind.

These weaknesses should include more than just your work offering. It's easy to focus on ensuring you deliver your service – working *in* your business – and keep your fingers crossed when it comes to working *on* your business. Perhaps you are late invoicing or slow to raise proposals or quotes. This can prove troublesome for clients and has the potential to lose you work. Identifying a weakness is the first step in addressing it.

If you do event- or project-based work that is very intensive and has a fast turnaround, you can come out the other side and find that you've no work, nothing in the pipeline and no idea who might be contracting for what and when. Even if you are really good at your work you would need to address the weakness of having nothing filling your pipeline whilst you are on a project.

A line producer I work with has great strengths in the early stages of production, preparing budgets, finding solutions to challenges, getting a crew together and delivering on the filming and getting the programme into the edit. However, her weakness comes to the fore when it comes to the final step, the final paperwork. Getting that done and delivered is harder than getting my kids to tidy their bedrooms. This is a real problem, not least because it's what clients have as the final memory of their work together. It's not something I would want my clients remembering me for. It is a major weakness.

It's not enough just to be good at what you actually do; you are a freelancer and you have to run all aspects of your operation yourself. Successful freelancers do this, and they do it efficiently as a part of their work ethos.

Opportunities are all the things you *could* be doing. You may not at this stage know how to achieve them, but for now it's important to acknowledge their existence. You can worry about the practicalities later. Opportunities come from the wider environment in which you operate, so you need to keep on top of what is happening in the sectors you work in. New developments and changes in social or economic conditions have the potential to make your offering more attractive.

Perhaps you can see an opportunity in a sector that you think could really benefit from your services. Perhaps there are new markets opening up that will demand your skills or perhaps technology and remote working mean you have a wider potential customer base than before. Consider how you can position yourself to take advantage of these new opportunities. What about political, environmental and legal conditions – do these offer up opportunities for your services?

Almost every company now, irrespective of sector, has a social media presence, and many don't need a full-time specialist to create their content. Thus, a whole new freelancing opportunity has arisen for social media content creators. Think about what you know about your offering and what is happening in the marketplace. Consider how technology is changing the way you work, what new opportunities it is bringing and how you can embrace it to offer an enhanced service. If you have recently completed work for a new client in a new industry sector, then treat it as an opportunity to look for further work in that sector using what you've just done as a calling card.

Threats can be the hardest to identify. They are the aspects of the wider environment that have the potential to stymie your work. They are, if you like, the risks to your offering. What are the changes that pose a risk to you?

Maybe there is a risk of obsolescence to your offering: can you be so experienced that companies no longer want your services? Perhaps your charges are now deemed too high for some sectors of your traditional work so you may be about to lose a chunk of your clients. (However, this could also mean an opportunity with a whole new set of clients. In the same way that strengths and weaknesses are intertwined so are opportunities and threats.)

If you can identify a threat to your business, you can usually figure out a way to neutralize it and/or turn it into a new opportunity. As a trainer and facilitator, a common threat to my work – especially in universities – is financial pressure where an institution lacks the budget to hire external people to deliver training or visiting-speaker sessions. This is where I need to work hard to demonstrate to the decision makers and influencers why I bring value and so ensure I continue to be booked.

Having completed this analysis on your 'company' you should now have a much clearer insight into what it is that makes it special, what its unique selling proposition is. Your USP goes hand in hand with your brand values that you identified earlier.

CUSTOMERS

Once you have identified a genuine need for your services you can start to visualize your potential clients. To set up a successful freelance operation it is vital to understand who your potential customers are – your customer 'pool' – as this will inform your marketing plan and will help you tailor your approach.

You will probably be selling your services to other businesses rather than direct to consumers, and the first step in identifying your customers is a visualization exercise.

Think about who your clients will be, what they will look like. Take some time to draw a picture of your ideal customer (space for this is provided on page 58). Go into as much detail as possible. It's not about great artwork, it's about visualizing who these potential customers are and where you can find them. Ask yourself as many questions as you can about your customer pool.

You are very likely to have an image in your head about what your customers look like. You want to visualize what sort of companies they are – large or small, public sector or private sector – and which industries they are in.

I expect you will be able to visualize more than one type of customer. This is very common. It just means a little more work and drawing at this stage as you need to visualize each type of customer.

As you sketch out what your customers look like, visualize the answers to these questions:

- Who are they?
- Where are they?
- When might they want your services?
- How do you talk to them?
- Does your service satisfy a need for your customer?
- How much will they pay for your service?
- Who is the decision maker?

WHO ARE YOUR CUSTOMERS?

Ask yourself what sort of companies your customers might be – large or small, public or private sector. Is there a specific industry sector or do you work across different ones? If you're in more than one, then you have different types of customers, so go into as much detail as possible about each.

For example, if you are a community fundraiser then your customers are likely to be in the 'not for profit' or charity sector. However, these organizations can be large or small, which makes the people and their needs different, so you would treat them as different types of customers.

WHERE ARE THEY?

This could be taken literally as, 'Are they local or international?' but it's more than just that. 'Where are they?' also concerns their relative position in their industry and whether they operate online or offline (or both). Think about where your customers need to be.

WHEN MIGHT THEY WANT YOUR SERVICES?

Your offering might be seasonal. There might be specific points in the client's business cycle where they require your type of services. If you are an events planner then you'll be particularly busy over the summer months and in the lead-up to Christmas, when significantly more events take place.

If you already have clients then think about where in their business cycle they call you in for work. It's also worth asking yourself whether they contact you at the right time or whether you could add further value by working with them at an earlier or later stage in their cycle.

HOW DO YOU 'TALK' TO THEM?

This question asks about the best way to approach your customers. More specifically, how do you think your client wants to be marketed to?

Remember, even though you are targeting companies, *people* work at companies and *people* make decisions. Your task is to get in front of the *right person* at the *right time* with the *right message*. There are always going to be others with the same technical expertise as you so you need something more: an 'edge' that provides additional value to your client or somehow differentiates you so you can build and maintain a loyal client base.

Remember, too, that the people you are dealing with want to do their work well, and feel valued and appreciated for doing it. Sometimes the edge you need is as simple as just being nice to deal with and having a sense of humour.

Never forget you're dealing with people. Make it easy for them to like you as a person.

DOES YOUR CUSTOMER HAVE A 'WANT' OR A 'NEED' YOUR SERVICE WILL SATISFY?

Think about the difference between 'nice to have' and 'need to have'. Consider whether your services sit on the 'nice to have' side or the 'need to have' side. I learned this when I ran Girls Angels – the types of customers I was looking to attract didn't 'need' to get a motorbike licence. They *wanted* to, but they didn't *need* to. If you can define your service in terms of being something that a company *needs* rather than a 'nice to have' you will make your proposition more attractive.

MY CUSTOMER(S) LOOK LIKE . . .

HOW MUCH WILL THEY PAY FOR YOUR SERVICE?

There's a lot more detail on this in Chapter 5, 'Valuing Yourself'. For now, just consider what intelligence you have already about how much your potential customers will pay for your services.

WHO IS THE DECISION MAKER?

This is important. You will often be dealing with more than one person, especially if you are targeting larger organizations, and each person will have a different role. When pitching to these customers it is vital to understand the roles that different individuals play in the decision-making process *before* you try to win the sale.

Reflect on the different companies you have interacted with – can you identify the following roles (some people may take on more than one role):

- initiator
- influencer
- decider
- buyer
- user

In order to negotiate your way through and make a sale, you need to understand quickly who does what and importantly who will support you in getting the work.

The **initiator** is the person who's initiated the conversation between you and the company. Now that you are coming in for a meeting it is your opportunity to assess (if you haven't already) what their role is within the organization – are they solely the initiator or do they wear other hats too?

The **influencer** is the person who can act as your in-house sponsor – they will (you hope) be your advocate within the company.

The **decider** is the person who has the ultimate responsibility to make the decision about whether you should be contracted for the work. This is the person you need to convince. Now you're at the meeting you need to ascertain whether they are at the table. If not, then your route in will be via the influencer. You're not going to make a sale unless the decider is present, so don't try.

The **buyer** is the person who pays for your services. Often they will be in a financial role and show more concern about price than about quality or added value of your work. They will always know of someone cheaper than you. That, after all, is their job.

This is where your values and *client-focussed thinking* come to the fore as you will need to convince the influencer and the decider that they should book *you* because this is a *value-added decision*, not a price one (more on these concepts later in the chapter).

The **user** is the person who is the ultimate consumer of your work. This could be someone or a team in an organization or it could be a customer of the organization contracting you.

By understanding the dynamics of decision making you can streamline your marketing activities by focussing on the key people in the organization you are targeting and their individual agendas to ensure a smooth pathway for your pitch.

CUSTOMER AWARENESS

Once you've got a visual idea of who your ideal customers are, the next question to ask is if they are aware of your existence. The ALTR model is a useful tool for examining this:

- **Awareness** – the percentage of your customer pool who are aware of your services.
- **Liking** – the percentage of your customer pool who like your services.
- **Trial** – the percentage of your customer pool who have tried your services.
- **Repeat** – the percentage of your customer pool who have come back for more.

Your customer pool consists of all the potential customers you have identified. It may be that you struggle to give a specific percentage for each answer – what you are looking for is where you estimate the percentage drops off sharply.

If you are a new starter in the industry or new to freelancing, awareness in your pool will be low, so you would need to start by getting the message out about you and your services.

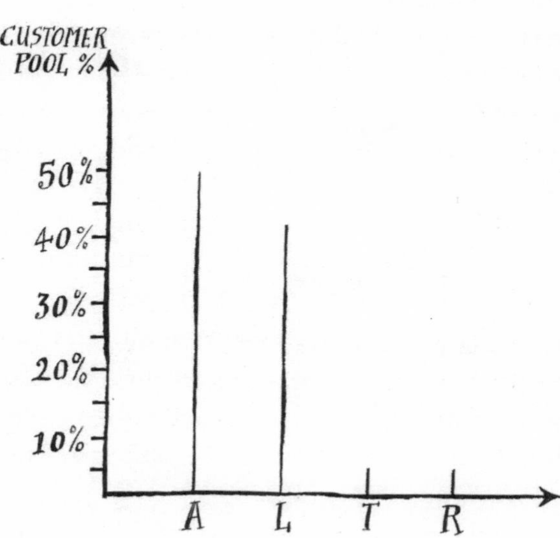

If, as in the figure here, you think that 42 per cent of your customer pool like the services you offer but only 5 per cent have tried them then you need to focus your marketing on moving people from liking to trying.

If no one is coming back for more, look at the reasons why they aren't. Reflect on the work you've done to understand why they aren't buying again. It's much more expensive to find a new customer than to keep an existing one.

If you've ever negotiated on your mobile-phone tariff at the end of your contract, you'll know how good a deal you can strike for an upgrade if you suggest you might leave your provider. The reason they want to keep you is their ARPU (average revenue per user). In simple terms, it's much more expensive to attract a new customer than keep an existing one. This applies to your work too; it will cost you a great deal of time and therefore money to find new clients, so keeping your existing clients happy and keeping in touch with them is going to be highly cost effective.

For those who deal with standalone projects, where repeat business is not part of the business model, then customer acquisition will be a key part of your marketing strategy. This was the case when I was running Girls Angels. The majority of customers just came to get their motorbike licence. Once they'd passed their test, that was it.

However, I did use our customer base for one essential activity: gaining recommendations. Word of mouth was a very important source of new customers, so I worked hard to ensure that every customer had a great experience and then went on to tell their friends and colleagues. And, let's face it, who's not going to tell their friends and colleagues when they have a shiny new motorbike and want to show it off?

GOOD CUSTOMERS

Now let's look at what makes a good customer. This sounds like a trite question on the surface but for me it goes to the heart of understanding your customers. Ultimately, I want all my customers to be good customers and it's up to me to define what 'good' means to me and my work.

Take some time to consider what makes a good customer for you and where your red lines are. Those points beyond which you won't go and where a customer stops being a good customer.

Characteristics of good customers could include:

- Paying on time.
- Paying a proper rate.
- Being easy and efficient to deal with.
- Recommending your work to new clients.
- Being nice people to work with.
- Offering interesting, high-profile or challenging work.

Now look at which of these characteristics are must-haves for you. If cash flow is critical to your work, then you might make paying on time a red-line characteristic in that you won't work with them again if they let you down. That may sound harsh but the amount of time that you can tie up chasing payment can be substantial.

Now look at all these characteristics and consider how many need to be in place for you to deem a customer 'good'. Try setting the bar at three criteria out of six. Look closely – your favourite customers may not turn out to be your best customers.

A good customer for me is someone who . . .

....

....

....

....

....

....

To be a good customer they need to fulfil a minimum of ____ traits.

However, before you consider dropping a client, think whether you might be able to retrain them. If they are regular clients and you like working with them perhaps you can discuss whether there are ways of managing their payments to you better – they might be horrified to learn that their finance department is not paying you on time. A grown-up conversation is a good way to start and can often turn a possible bad customer into a great one. For more on dealing with late payments see Chapter 13 'Pacing Yourself for a Marathon'.

Now you know what a good customer looks like you can have some fun trying to turn all your customers into good ones.

One freelancer I know won't quote until he has met the client. He knows he can tell from one meeting how challenging the client relationship is going to be and therefore he prices accordingly.

I'm sure you'd feel better about working with your more difficult clients were you to charge them extra. *Money changes everything*, so think about how you can initiate that conversation. Or do as my colleague does and quote accordingly.

At the other end of the scale, another freelancer I know will meet a client only once they've agreed his rates in principle so he doesn't waste time in pointless negotiation. Only you can decide which path is right for you.

Ultimately you may find that some customers are just not a good fit for you. It goes back to your values. If you are someone who thrives in a commercial environment, then you are likely to find that the not-for-profit sector is not a good match.

This is not a reflection on you and how *you* operate. You aren't inferior because you can't work well with an organization that has very different values from your own. Equally, it isn't a reflection on the client. When a mismatch occurs, use it as a learning experience and target customers who share your values and operate in a similar way to you.

Now that you have a full picture of who your customers are or might be, it is time to move on to the last of the 3Cs: competition.

COMPETITION

No matter what it is that you do, there will be others operating in the same space as you and the chances are at least some will be fishing in the same pool of customers.

First, don't worry. There will always be competition. It's a fact of life, but people do get worked up about it – and there's no need. When I ran Girls Angels the owner of a local motorbike training school saw us as a new competitor, but I could see that our focus was on a different customer segment so, in reality, we were not competing against each other.

Another fact of life is that there will always be people cheaper than you. Whilst it's true that most markets are sensitive to price, they are generally more sensitive to other factors such as quality and timeliness, so don't try to win work by being the cheapest.

Finally, never *ever* bad-mouth your competition. It's not attractive, word will get round and customers don't like it. Plus, you never know when the opportunity might arise for you to recommend each other or collaborate in the future.

As with the first two Cs, the way to cope with competition is to analyse it, and in order to analyse it properly you need to start with sector mapping.

SECTOR MAPPING

Sector mapping pulls together a detailed picture of the ecosystem you are working in or wish to work in. It helps build a picture of how many others might be operating in the same or a similar space. Starting with the macro picture, you can map the business process into four phases: creating, making, distributing and using.

The more you understand where your services sit at the macro level the easier it is to understand where your customer's pain is *and how you can solve their problem through your services*. Your offering can sit at any point in this continuum and can also straddle two adjoining phases.

For example, when working as a producer, I am firmly in the making phase. The *creators* hire my services to make the film and my services are complete when it is made and I deliver it to the client who then moves on to *distributing*.

If you have a portfolio career and find that you work in both creating and making, be aware that these require different skills and mindsets so it can be hard to work on both at the same time.

Within each phase there can be many other people creating, making or distributing alongside you. This is particularly true of making, where it can take a whole range of skills to transform an idea into commercial reality.

Now think vertically about how your industry works. What I mean by this is think about *who you are working for* and then *who they are working for*. Perhaps you have people working under you.

Picture it as a ladder: a good example of this is the ecosystem around a digital marketer doing the online strategy for an exhibition. Their *vertical* ladder would have a PR manager and a marketing director above them with PR assistants and social media assistants below them.

Now consider your ladder: who's above you and who is below you, and how you all operate and interact. Using the blank put yourself on the centre rung and then add in all the people who are above you and all the people below you.

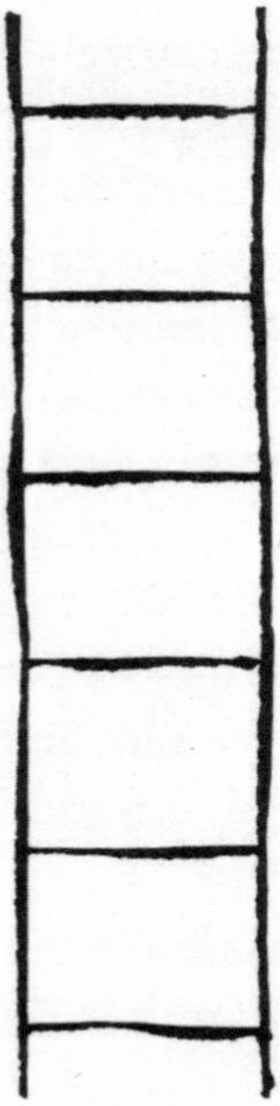

Once you've done that draw a ladder sideways and think about the *process* involved in the work you do. First consider what processes are involved in the work the digital marketer does. Their *horizontal* ladder would show that they come into the process during the planning of the exhibition, where they would put together an online marketing strategy, but the main part of their work would be delivered in the run-up to the exhibition launch and whilst the exhibition was open to the public. Once the exhibition has closed it is unlikely there would be a need for their services, until the next one.

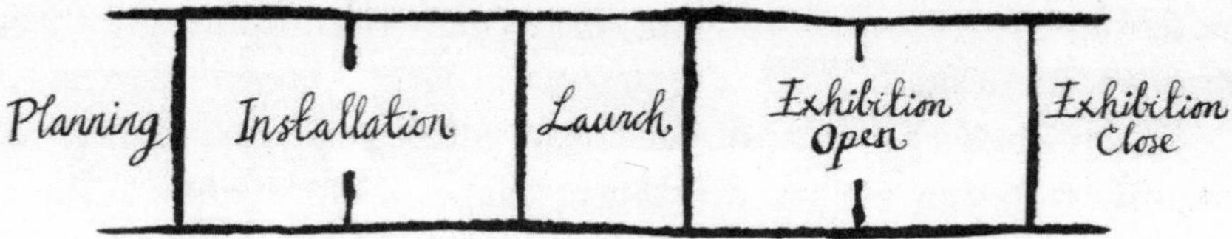

Using the blank draw your ecosystem on the horizontal ladder. Think about the full process your client goes through in delivering their work and where you fit into that.

Sector mapping shows you the links between the roles. It helps you visualize the big picture and all the people needed for a business to deliver its entire services to its customers. You are likely to be one small part of this activity for your clients. Sector mapping can help you understand how and where you fit into the picture.

I find this mapping exercise really helpful in understanding the ecosystem that surrounds each piece of work I do, how many people have input into a project and all the parties and skills needed to deliver it. It also helps me to understand the steps and processes involved in getting a project from an idea to a customer and to see the bigger picture about where I fit in.

Now that you have this intelligence you can start to look at where your competition is lurking.

DIRECT COMPETITION

Your direct competitors are the people (freelancers or companies) who are operating in the same space as you. If there are a lot, you'll need to look at how you can differentiate your offering for potential clients so that you can make them value you more than your competition.

When analysing your direct competition your first task is to identify who they are and do your research on them. Look at their websites, their social media, their company filings and any other information you can discover about them. See if you can find out who their customers are. Arm yourself with as much information as possible about what they do and why their customers choose them. The more you know, the better equipped you will be to articulate in your marketing efforts why customers should choose you. You want to make clear how you will add much more value to them than others will. Don't forget, the only person who wins a price war is the customer.

If you work as a freelance camera operator in a studio or on an outside broadcast, for example, you are likely to be one of a team of camera operators covering that project so you would already be collaborating with your competition. This can at first glance seem like the worst of all worlds: you have to work with your direct competitors, and they might learn all your tricks and put you out of business. But for me this is nonsense, short-term thinking.

Your clients want to know they are working with people that they can trust to deliver and are good to work with. All the people on this job are people they trust to deliver. So, you need to ensure you are that person *all the time*. Especially when you are working with your direct competition or rather – in this instance – collaborating with them.

Think about it: a potential new client contacts you to see if you are free to do a piece of work. You'd really like to accept, but you just can't fit it in. You could take the short-term view that you can't do it, never mind, and press on with the work you're already booked for. Or you can take the big-picture, longer-term view: tell them you're sorry you're busy but that there is someone you could recommend instead, and you would be happy to connect them up. You are solving a problem for your would-be client and making their life easy.

They are almost certainly going to call you again because you are helpful, and they will remember that. You're someone who thinks about them, not yourself. Of course, you must make sure the person you recommend is good, but most importantly also make sure that person knows the recommendation came from you. Human nature will make them want to return the favour.

As you can see, even though there may be a large number of other freelancers in direct competition with you, it is still beneficial to build relationships with them. Collaboration is a great tactic for neutralizing your direct competition.

Another example concerns a network of freelance costumiers who would send work each other's way at busy times. One member realized she was missing out on the bigger jobs because clients assumed that, as a solo freelancer, she lacked the capacity to handle them. So she joined forces with one of her freelance colleagues and together they set up a company. This allowed them to greatly increase their capacity and to pitch for and win much bigger jobs. Their joint company has gone from strength to strength and they now work on major international projects.

Aside from collaboration, another factor to examine within your industry is whether your sector is growing or shrinking. A growing sector usually generates both more work and more people trying to win it – increased competition.

Consider how that will affect you and how you can ensure that you will maintain a full schedule. Situations such as these where you have deeper relationships with your clients and the right approach will stand you in good stead. A growing industry can also signal approaching fragmentation, where sectors splinter off and become their own micro-specialism. It is worth examining whether this is happening around you.

The camera operator I mentioned earlier saw an increasing number of theatrical productions being filmed for wider distribution (cinema, TV or online), and by dint of being involved early now has a great deal of experience in the specifics of realizing these projects. He is now a key player in the ecosystem of production companies, producers and film crew who are specializing in this field.

A sector that appears to be shrinking might, in reality, be fragmenting and specializing like the example above. If so, think about which of these fragments you have expertise in and look at how those are evolving.

If your sector truly is shrinking, there is likely to be an outflow of workers looking to find alternative work because the opportunities are drying up. Note that I say are drying up, not have dried up. Sectors rarely completely disappear; if anything, they get more specialized and more technical. Think about the 'I'-shaped people from Chapter 2. This is where the depth of experience (the length of your 'I') becomes important as there will be fewer suppliers to compete with, and if you take this to the extreme it can also push up prices as the supply of expertise dwindles. So, don't rush to jump off the ship just yet, but maybe think about seeking some new opportunities.

Now consider what happens if you find that you are doing something very different from other people, so there is almost no direct competition. It sounds great, but it has its own challenges. It is likely that many of your potential customers won't really understand what it is that you do and why they should buy into it. Chances are you will find that you spend more time educating your client about this broader new opportunity than discussing your specific offering.

A good example of this was back in the mid-2000s when I was working with a director pitching web videos when the technology was not as established as it is now. Our company had several pitches with large educational institutions who were considering using video content on their website and for wider communications.

What happened in the meetings was that more time would be spent discussing how and why video worked and what the opportunity was for them rather than pitching why they should choose our company. It was a two-stage sales process – first educate the client on *why* it was a good idea to spend money on video for their website and then why they should spend it on *us*. Fortunately, we found that once the client bought into why they needed video they tended to buy into us too.

So, if you find yourself in a new and emerging industry, remember that your potential customers may need you to start at the beginning and help them understand what it is that you can really do for them. The good news is that once you've got them hooked, they are likely to be loyal to you.

INDIRECT COMPETITION

Indirect competition arises when you are competing with others who don't do what you do but are chasing the same customers' budgets.

When I was running my motorbike training school, I was competing for customers' disposable income along with thousands of indirect competitors. By being aware that customers might be choosing between a bike licence and – say – a holiday or a new outfit meant our marketing messages were geared very much towards depicting our service as an aspirational activity rather than a commodity.

A freelance workshop facilitator I know talks eloquently on this when she pitches for education projects. She explains it thus: if pupil literacy is a challenge for a head teacher, they might look to bring in some external experienced facilitators to work with pupils. She reminds them that, although the only requirement is that the intervention improves literacy, it would be a nice bonus if the kids enjoyed the sessions as well.

There are myriad ways in which a facilitator can tackle this challenge. In this situation you would be competing against people who are all offering different solutions to the same problem. The question then becomes how you can ensure that your way is the one that is most attractive.

By being aware that you aren't just up against your direct competition but a much wider group – your indirect competition – you can present your offering to take this into account. Consider what your expertise brings to the work that others can't. Consider your hard and soft skills and any incidental benefits. This is where you can make yourself stand out from the crowd.

So, in thinking about your competition, it's important to

remember that it's not all daggers at dawn. Yes, there are always going to be freelancers that you will be pitching against for work. But they also have the potential to become your collaborators, a source of referrals and your community and network.

Who else knows better what it's like to freelance than another freelancer?

3Cs SUMMARY

You've covered a huge part of your market research:

- You've looked inside **yourself** at your company and identified the good and the not so good (**strengths** and **weaknesses**) so you know what you need to work on.
- You've identified **opportunities** and **threats** to your work.
- You have an idea of **who** your customers are, **what** they look like and **where** you can find them.
- You've looked at the wider marketplace and what your **direct** and **indirect competition** is.

It's time now to start *organizing* that market research into customer-focussed thinking.

This is where you explain what you do in terms of 'Why me?'

WHAT VERSUS WHY

The author and motivational speaker Simon Sinek talks eloquently about this in his book *Start with Why*.

What provides a **factual understanding** of you to your client.

Why is a **differentiator**.

What tries to convince clients based on facts but *why* connects with their heart. The challenge is to find your *why*.

Apple are the experts at selling on the *why* and not the *what*. A great example is the success of the iPod over mp3 players. When mp3 players first came out they were sold at a premium – but as more companies entered the market prices dropped. They were being sold on the 'what' and treated as a commodity.

When Apple launched the iPod they sold it on the basis of *why* you needed it – because you could have a thousand songs in your pocket. They won hearts and minds and were able to maintain a high price.

Now it's time to articulate your *why*.

WHY ME?

As you start to devise a strategy for servicing your customers it's important that you think in terms of why your offering will benefit them.

It's not that you are changing what you are offering, just how you talk about it. You need to explain **why your offering benefits them** rather than just telling them what you do and assuming they'll somehow figure out for themselves why they will benefit.

You might think that's a no-brainer and stating the obvious, but so many people fail to do it. *Connecting the dots for the customer to make it an easy decision for them to engage your services is vital.*

To give you an example of client-focussed thinking in action, I worked with two young women who were passionate filmmakers and wanted to sell filmmaking workshops into schools. They were convinced that pupils would really enjoy learning to make films, so they set up meetings with local schools and they received a lot of interest. The schools agreed the pupils would enjoy the workshops, but the challenge was that there was no funding for such an activity.

The women were understandably frustrated, they were building awareness and schools liked their proposition, but they couldn't get anyone to try it out. When I probed further it became apparent that in their pitches they were only talking and thinking in terms of *what*. Basically, they were saying: '[*Our company*] *sells filmmaking workshops for children to schools,'* but they were giving no reason for the client to buy what they were offering.

When I asked them about the why, they told me it was very simple: when pupils are making films, they also use many other important skills. Writing scripts helps with literacy. Research helps with literacy and computer skills. They have to make presentations, which gives them confidence. And they have to work as a team. I asked if schools have funding to improve any of those areas. 'Of course!' they said. 'Literacy is a key challenge in many schools.'

The penny had dropped. They were now starting to think about their *why*. Now their pitch could be: *'Are you looking to improve literacy with your pupils? If yes, then we have the solution – our filmmaking workshops do just that . . .'*

The schools could now understand how the workshops benefited the curriculum and were able to allocate part of their literacy enhancement budget. The filmmaking workshops weren't just workshops – they were a solution to the school's problem of how to improve pupil literacy. The filmmakers' pitch was now client-focussed because they understood *why* the school needed their offering.

Going further, they were also able to target their marketing activity more effectively because they could consult Department for Education reports to identify which schools were struggling with literacy and so were more likely to be receptive to their pitch.

The result of this shift in their marketing strategy was dramatic, even though in many ways nothing had changed – they were doing the work they had always envisaged they wanted to do. The big difference was that they now understood *why* their customers would buy from them.

Go back to page 45, where you described **'This is what I do'**. Using this as a starting point, write down under **'Why me?'** all the reasons that customers should choose you. Again, if you have a portfolio of offerings then you'll need to do this for each distinctive strand of work you do.

Think carefully about what it is that your clients value and will

WHY ME?

make them keep choosing you. Consider all aspects of your relationship with your client.

Remember that people don't buy drills because they want a drill. *They buy a drill because they need holes.* So, how do you sell them faster, neater, cleaner holes?

Another way to unlock this thinking is to ask yourself what the problem is for your customer that you are trying to solve and think about how you can explain yourself as the solution to their problem.

A good indication that you are talking to your customers in terms of *why* is when you find yourself saying phrases like 'I do __________________ and that means __________________ for you'.

Always remember, you are not at the centre of your work, your customers are. And you don't always need to be able to do everything yourself – know when to bring in partners and build alliances.

Now that you've done this exercise you should be able to communicate your offering in a client-focussed way. Be clear on what your vision is and make sure you can articulate it simply and consistently.

More on this later – but first it's time to approach from a different angle – a reality check on the numbers to make sure the financials of your freelance proposition will work for you.

4.

IT'S ALL ABOUT THE MONEY!

Money is naturally one of the biggest concerns for any freelancer, and it doesn't matter whether you consider yourself as being good with numbers or not: to be successful you have to take ownership of your finances and know what you need to earn to survive. The good news is that it's not too difficult to do.

Your 'value' in the marketplace is not easy to assess, but there are strategies that will help you to determine the correct pricing level for where you are now. As you gain experience and skills you can raise your rate. You might also charge different rates for different aspects of your work, or for different clients or sectors.

But before you work out what you think you might be able to charge, you have to work out how much you need to earn to live the life you want to lead. You must also consider how to manage your regular outgoings on an irregular income.

HOW MUCH DO I REALLY NEED TO LIVE ON?

When was the last time that you properly analysed your spending? You'll be amazed by how the small things add up over the course of a year.

The first thing you need to calculate is the cost to you of living your life as you want to live it. This is your living budget. You can use the table on page 80 to record what you spend as you work it out. Write down each item's weekly or monthly cost and then multiply by either 52 or 12 to calculate the annual total. The table brings together five major areas of expenditure – Household, Transport, Personal, Financial and Miscellaneous – and any income you receive that doesn't come from freelancing. The difference between the two is the income you need to earn as a freelancer.

HOUSEHOLD COSTS

Your largest monthly outlay will probably be your rent or mortgage, followed by local taxes such as council tax and TV licence in the UK, utilities such as water, gas and electricity, and insurance for your property and its contents. Most of us have home broadband, perhaps with associated TV subscription and landline costs, as well as a mobile phone contract. Include any other essential costs such as boiler servicing. If you have any additional household outlays specific to your personal circumstances, add those in also. Be as accurate as you can.

If what you are paying is likely to increase soon, then make allowances for that. For example, if you are living with family currently and paying little or no rent but plan to move to a new location for work, it's sensible to factor in that new level of expenditure.

TRANSPORT COSTS

You have to be able to get out and about. Put in this section all the costs associated with your transportation. Include any finance or leasing costs you pay on your vehicle, road tax, insurance and any parking and servicing costs. Allow for consumables, such as new tyres. Divide your annual mileage by your car's estimated miles per litre to find your expected annual fuel consumption. Think about whether your annual mileage will increase or fall when you become a freelancer.

If you plan to use your car for work you must make sure that your insurance policy covers own-business use. See the Insurance appendix on page 239 for more details.

If you use public transport regularly, estimate how much this costs you per week or per month.

PERSONAL COSTS

This is where most people get the biggest surprises regarding what they spend. It can be a real eye-opener.

Whether your guilty pleasure is a daily pint, a luxury coffee or a smoothie, it's the incidental expenses such as these that really add up. I'm as guilty as the next person of liking 'proper' coffee – I must average five per week, and that's before I buy a sandwich or some sushi for lunch if I am out at meetings. If you assume each coffee costs £3, that's £15 per week. And then if you add in another £15 average per week for food on the run then it's £30 per week, or over £1,500 per year IN CAFÉS ALONE.

Think about what you spend your money on. What's your snack of choice – Red Bull and a sausage roll or sushi and coconut water? Think about how much they cost and how often you buy them and note it all down.

In the personal section, also think about your spend on groceries and household supplies. Include your weekly shop plus any takeaways and other incidental food purchases.

'Entertainment' includes eating out, going to the cinema (don't forget to include the popcorn as well as the cinema ticket) or other social events such as the theatre, ice skating, sporting events etc. Whatever your entertainment of choice, note it down and add it up.

LIVING BUDGET

Estimated Outgoings	Weekly x 52	Monthly x 12	Annual Total
Household			
Mortgage and/or rent			
Council tax			
Water			
Gas/electricity			
Broadband/TV/landline			
Insurance – home and contents			
Mobile phone			
Other – household			
Transport			
Car – financial			
Car – insurance/road tax			
Fuel			
Parking			
Servicing and maintenance			
Public transport			
Other – transport			
Personal			
Groceries/household supplies			
Entertainment (meals, drinks, cinema etc.)			
Health and fitness (membership/classes)			
Technology (laptop, tablet, games console etc.)			
Holiday expenditure			
Gifts for friends and family			
Clothing and beauty			
Books, magazines, subscriptions			
Other – snacks and incidentals			

Estimated Outgoings	Weekly x 52	Monthly x 12	Annual Total
Financial			
Savings plan			
Pension			
Other – financial products			
Other			
Other – expenditure			
Annual subtotal			
Contingency 10–15 % of Annual subtotal			
Total outgoings			
Income (non-freelance work)			
Income from family or partner			
Other income (exclude freelance work)			
Total income			
Living budget = Total outgoings – Total income			

Don't forget the extras. For example, if you have a gym membership you may need to add in the cost of classes and/or extra drinks and snacks you buy whilst you are there to see the real cost of keeping fit.

What about the technology you own for your personal use such as a laptop, tablet or games console? These are all big-ticket items when it comes to upgrading them.

Another item on the personal list is holidaying. Think about how often you take holidays or weekend breaks. Think about what you spend on this well-earned downtime. Don't forget to include all those incidentals – duty-free at the airport and yet more coffees and snacks on long drives or train journeys.

Gifting is another often-neglected expense to include in your personal budgeting. Consider how much you spend on presents for friends and family on their birthdays and other occasions. It's important to show your loved ones you care by buying them gifts – but it all adds up.

What about the shopping you do for yourself on clothes, shoes, beauty products and technology? Or book and magazine subscriptions? This is all part of living the life you want to live and needs to be part of the calculations.

Finally, in the 'other' section think about anything else you regularly spend money on. Perhaps you enjoy karate or photography in your spare time. Whatever it is, it all costs, so note it down. The more accurate you can be, the better.

At this point in my workshops participants start to look a little grey as they realize how much they are spending. They immediately renounce the material world and declare that they will live a frugal existence from now on. No more coffees, no more new clothes and so on. But that's not the intention of this exercise. *It's a reality check*. It is not a judgement.

The only way to know what you need to earn to support the life you enjoy living is to know *precisely* how you spend your money.

If as a result of this exercise you rein in some of your spending, that is your personal choice. Just remember that, like crash diets, going über-frugal suddenly is very unlikely to be a sustainable option. Your spending might drop for a while, but will probably pick up again as you start to run out of the supplies you had to hand already.

I try to operate on a nice-to-have vs need-to-have basis, and when I don't have the money in my account, I don't spend on the nice-to-have items.

FINANCIAL COSTS

Put in here the costs of any credit card debt or loans. If they will be paid up within the year then just add the total in the 'Annual' column; if they are longer term then put in your weekly or monthly payments.

Do you have a regular savings plan? If so, you'll need to consider whether or how to keep this up when your income is irregular. Perhaps change from a monthly amount to a percentage of each payment you receive. You may also have a contributory pension. Note down all these and any other financial outlays in this section.

OTHER COSTS

The final expenditure section covers any further personal spending that hasn't already been covered. Think about any other regular payments you make, such as childcare, school fees or medical plans.

Even though you've tried to factor in everything for the year, there will always arise unexpected costs. I like to allow a contingency of 10–15 per cent of annual outgoings for these as there's no knowing what might break down and it's prudent to be prepared for sudden and unexpected costs such as a new TV or washing machine.

INCOME (NON-FREELANCE WORK AND OTHER INCOME)

In this section, write down any income you earn outside your freelance work – perhaps you have a part-time job or an income from renting out a room in your house. If so, note it down. If you live with a partner, friends or family and you have put your entire household outgoings into the table put any contribution they make in the table.

LIVING BUDGET

Now, check carefully that you've put the monthly and weekly figures in the correct columns – it's easily confused. Next, add up what you've entered in the table for all your outgoings (including contingency), then add up all your income.

You can now calculate your living budget figure for the year by subtracting total income from total outgoings. You can then divide by 52 or 12 to give you an idea of your average living budget spend per week or month. However, these are only averages – your income will vary month by month, so you'll have to keep on top of how much cash you have at any one time. Cash flow is covered in Chapter 13, 'Pacing Yourself for a Marathon'.

Unfortunately, that isn't the end of the story. This figure is what needs to be left over **after** you've paid all your taxes and business expenses. But before considering those obligations, there is one more area to look at: the tools of your trade.

TOOLS OF THE TRADE

Strictly speaking, this final section is neither personal nor ongoing business spending; rather it's the one-off start-up business expenses you will incur at the outset of your freelance career that will enable you to launch your brand and buy in any equipment and materials you need in order to deliver your services.

Whilst these are usually tax deductible, at this stage they are real costs that you must pay from your personal funds, which is why they are included here. (If you are an established freelancer and are already covering these costs from your business income you can leave this section blank.)

To do your work in the first instance you'll almost certainly need your own laptop or PC and associated software plus a domain name and email address. This may also be the first time you will be responsible for your own technology, which can be a daunting experience. Be prudent. At this stage you may not need top-of-the-range equipment, but also think ahead as you'll need whatever you buy to last for a good amount of time. Consider any other equipment or software that you will have to purchase up front in order to do your work.

You'll need a mobile phone, but generally this is something you would have for personal use anyway. I've included it twice in the list, under 'household' and under 'tools of the trade'. If you decide to have a separate, work-only mobile, then you'd add it in to the latter section. If you are happy to use your personal phone for work you can leave that bit blank. There's a real split between freelancers who keep their work separate and turn the 'work' mobile off out-of-hours, and those who run only one phone.

On top of the equipment costs for your tools of the trade you might also need a stock of materials specific to your services. For example, a make-up artist will require make-up supplies before they can deliver their services. Stationery is another up-front expense: you'll at least need some business cards and perhaps some flyers or other marketing materials. You'll certainly need to factor in travel costs to get to client meetings to win work.

Tools of the trade	Weekly x 52	Monthly x 12	Annual Total
Equipment (laptop, printer, software and other specialist equipment)			
Materials			
Travel and subsistence			
TOTAL			

Add all this up and it will give you the amount you will need to find from your personal funds to finance your tools of the trade in addition to your living budget as you embark on your freelance career.

Now there are just two further areas of expenditure to consider in order to arrive at your 'need-to-earn' figure: business expenses and tax liability.

BUSINESS EXPENSES

The term 'business expenses' covers any legitimate expenditure incurred in the running of your business, from initial client meetings and pitches through to delivering projects and wrapping them up afterwards.

Every jurisdiction has its own rules and regulations regarding what you can claim and how to do it, but a good rule of thumb is to consider business expenses as those necessary for the performance of your work. *Business expenses are deducted from your total income before any taxes are calculated* – so it's in your interest to keep good records.

The exact details of what are considered business expenses do vary by country,* and an accountant is the best person to advise you on the specifics of your particular work in your jurisdiction, but most agree that the following are tax-deductible expenses:

- Advertising and marketing.
- Office supplies.
- Computer equipment and software.
- Travel and business subsistence.
- Home office.

There may well be others, dependent on your jurisdiction and your specific work.

You have calculated your start-up business expenses in tools of the trade alongside your living budget, now it's time to look at the ongoing business expenses you will incur in doing your work.

* For more specific information on the UK and other tax jurisdictions visit https://alisongrade.com/downloads

Estimate your business expenses in the table provided. Include your tools-of-the-trade figure. Don't forget that equipment and materials need replacing periodically, so it's a good idea to set something aside for that. It's worth doing an audit of your equipment and materials at this stage just to check if anything might need replacing or upgrading in the short to medium term and factor that in.

Business expenses	Weekly x 52	Monthly x 12	Annual total
Tools of the trade			
Advertising and marketing			
Office supplies			
Computer equipment and software			
Travel and business subsistence			
Home office			
Professional services (accountant/legal)			
Other (dependent on jurisdiction)			
TOTAL			

TAX LIABILITY

As soon as you start earning money you will need to put a proportion aside against any future liabilities for personal taxes (income tax and national insurance in the UK) and possibly those levied on sales (such as VAT in the UK and sales tax in the US).

At the end of each financial year you will need to file a tax return in the country where you are resident for tax purposes and then pay any personal taxes owing. Never forget that the tax element of what you charge customers is not yours to spend – **so don't spend it**. Tax authorities demand to be paid on time and will levy a penalty if you are late.

TURNOVER

Your annual turnover is the total amount you invoice your customers during the year. Think of your turnover as your 'sales target'. To live the life you want to lead according to your living budget, your turnover must equal or exceed the total of your living budget, business expenses and any tax liability.

This isn't a straightforward calculation. Tax rates vary in different jurisdictions and are usually income-dependent – the more you earn, the greater the proportion that goes in taxes. Plus, how you are set up legally can make a difference: sole trader, partnership, or incorporated. This is where an accountant who knows the local regulations is invaluable.

To get an indication, you will find useful resources online. For example in the UK, the HMRC website has a 'ready reckoner'* into which you can input the living-budget figure (your average weekly or monthly profit) you have calculated and it will work out your turnover (excluding business expenses) for you.

Turnover calculation	Annual
Living budget = total outgoings – total other income	
Estimated taxes owing (ready reckoner calculation)	
Business expenses	
Total = estimated annual turnover required	

Be aware this ready reckoner doesn't take into account any business expenses that your work may incur, so you'd need to add these to the figure it gives to get your turnover, but it's a good starting point.

Now that you've calculated your required turnover, you've

* For more specific information on the UK and other tax jurisdictions visit https://alisongrade.com/downloads

effectively set your minimum sales target for the year. Your next challenge is to work out your value in the marketplace so that you can come up with the hourly, daily and weekly rates necessary to achieve this level of sales. That will be the subject of the next chapter, but first, a look at managing your finances.

BANK ACCOUNTS

The most straightforward way to keep track of cash and your tax liabilities is by having three separate bank accounts.

- An account for your day-to-day **business banking** that your invoices are paid into and from which you can pay business expenses.
- An account for your day-to-day **personal spending**. Any money you pay yourself should be transferred from your business account to your personal account.
- A **savings account** for your estimated tax liability. You must put money aside **when every invoice is paid**. If you are registered for VAT, also known in some countries as GST (goods and services tax), you can use this account to park these monies too.

By separating out your income like this you should always have a snapshot of how much money is yours to spend and how much is earmarked for other purposes, helping to ensure you don't inadvertently spend what will be due to the tax authority later in the year.

All the major banks have business banking divisions and they'll usually offer sweeteners to open an account with them. Just don't expect them to have that much knowledge of freelancers; retail banks aren't set up to deal with them. The business bankers are there to service companies, and companies ask different questions and want different facilities, such as loans and investment, from you and me. Most freelancers I know use a business bank account to receive and make business-related payments and little else.

That said, there are some new financial technology (fintech) companies offering innovative approaches to business banking, some of which are primarily focussed on freelancers. Examples are Coconut in the UK and Joust in the USA.

ACCOUNTANTS

An accountant is a professional who acts on your behalf and is qualified to advise you on financial matters, prepare accurate financial accounts and ensure your taxes are paid properly and on time. It's not essential to hire an accountant to assist you with filing your annual accounts or tax return, but they can often save you more money than they cost as they know the rules regarding legitimate business expenses. In many jurisdictions their fees can be claimed against tax as a business expense.

Remember that the more preparation you do in terms of keeping good records the easier you make your accountant's job and the smaller the bill will be, so it's worth getting into the habit of keeping detailed records of your income and expenditure.

As you get busier you may also want to take into account the cost of **your** time: how much could you be earning in the time you spend on your accounts? At this point it might be more than an accountant would charge, and they'll probably do a better job as well.

FINANCIAL PRUDENCE

Financial prudence for me is keeping my 'financial self' healthy and keeping my spending within my means. If I don't have it, I don't spend it. It's also about knowing when you are in a position to plan for the future. I realize that this is an ideal, and not always achievable, but it's something you should keep in mind at all times.

When I talk about financial prudence to people who are

embarking on a freelance career, I explain the importance of using money in the most financially efficient way. For me this boils down to a *hierarchy of aims*:

- **AIM 1: ELIMINATE CREDIT-CARD DEBT**
  This is the most expensive kind of debt and should be paid off first. When you've done that:

- **AIM 2: THREE MONTHS' CASH FLOW**
  Start to save so that you have three months' worth of your living budget in your personal account that you can draw on at any time.

- **AIM 3: FUTUREPROOFING**
  Once you have three months' cash flow saved and know there is more work booked in, it is time to start embarking on longer-term savings and/or investment plans for the future.

It's up to you to fulfil these aims; you don't have an employer to do it for you.

Because being prudent with your finances is so important, let's just think about this a bit more.

Don't pay the credit-card company more than you have to in interest, even if that leaves you with less in your bank account in the short term. The credit card will still be there in an emergency and paying it off sooner will cost you less.

Then, once you have your debt paid off, you can start getting some short-term savings in place to act as a buffer against late payments and quieter periods. Again, this is the prudent thing to do. Three months is my suggestion, but you may feel more comfortable with a six-month cushion. It really depends on your personal circumstances and how much faith you have in your ability to find new work.

When you have an adequate buffer you can start to look at making some longer-term financial plans, such as a pension, being sure to take on only something you can afford. For these longer-term investments, developing a relationship with a qualified financial adviser who understands your work will be of great benefit.

Now you've done the hard work looking at what your life costs to live, it's time to come at the maths from the other direction and estimate your value in the marketplace.

5.

VALUING YOURSELF

Valuing yourself and estimating your daily rate is never a simple or straightforward task; in fact, it can be one of the hardest parts of being a freelancer.

Whilst understanding your monetary value is extremely important, it is not the only thing you should consider when assessing how much you can charge.

There are five factors that you should take into account:

1. Value based on your living budget.
2. Your level of experience.
3. Benchmarking – what do others earn for this work?
4. Industry sector variations.
5. Intended market for your work.

VALUE BASED ON LIVING BUDGET

A simple starting point for valuing yourself is to look at the relationship between your living budget and your value. In the previous chapter you estimated your annual turnover. If you have an idea of your daily or weekly rate then you can take that figure and divide it by your rate to see how many days or weeks in the year you need to work to break even – that is to have an income equal to your living budget.

Valuation based on an estimated rate:

£ ________________	÷ £ ________________	= £ ________________
est. annual turnover	est. daily rate	est. no. of paid days per year
£ ________________	÷ £ ________________	= £ ________________
est. annual turnover	est. weekly rate	est. no. of paid weeks per year

If you don't have an idea of your rate then another way to look at this is to work out a rate based on the number of paid working days in the year.

Valuation based on number of working days in year:

There are 52 weeks in the year: let's assume you take 4 weeks as holiday.

That leaves 48 weeks where you could be working.

Let's assume that you will only be working 5 days per week: 48 × 5 = 240 days.

Consider how many of these days is it realistic that you will be doing actual paid work: don't forget there are client meetings, paperwork and admin to factor in.

Let's assume that 50 per cent of these days are paid days = 24 weeks or 120 days.

Now calculate:

Estimated Annual Turnover ÷ 24 = £________ your weekly rate estimate

Estimated Annual Turnover ÷ 120 = £________ your daily rate estimate

How do these rates seem to you? About right? Too high? Too low? You can adjust how many paid working days you do in a year. These are very rough valuations, but if they show your estimated annual turnover is achievable only by working six days a week for fifty-two weeks per year there is a mismatch between your estimated earnings and your spending. But before you decide it's game over examine the other factors surrounding valuing yourself so you can build up a more complete picture.

YOUR LEVEL OF EXPERIENCE

Your level of experience is one of the most significant factors that influences your rate in the marketplace. Depending on which sector you work in, it will be easier or harder to calculate your value against it. Some sectors, such as TV production, have a hierarchical structure that makes this relatively simple as your value (your rate) is linked with your job title (credit) on the production. At each level there are loose bands for services, and as you gain more experience and move up the production ladder these will increase.

More broadly, you should be able to classify your level of experience quite easily. I break it down into four phases based on the number of years' experience you have in your role.

1. Just started (0–1 year)
2. Early stage (1–3 years)
3. Mid-career (3–5 years)
4. Experienced (5+ years)

This breakdown focusses on how long you've been doing the role you are currently doing – **not** how long you've been working in your sector. I was in the 'just started' category the first time I was hired as a producer, even though I had been working in the industry for well over ten years, because I hadn't been hired in that capacity before.

You are likely to find also that within each phase there are different micro-levels, particularly as you work your way up through early stage and mid-career. Consider where your level of experience lies in the work you do and how you can build up your experience and therefore the value you can offer to clients. This insight into your level of experience doesn't work in isolation; you also need to look at benchmarking.

BENCHMARKING – WHAT DO OTHERS EARN?

Benchmarking is a dark art, but if you start to interrogate a range of areas and pull all the information together you are likely to see a pattern emerge.

There are three main areas to delve into: **Sector resources, published opportunities** and **asking people**.

1. **SECTOR RESOURCES** are those put together by professional bodies such as a union or a trade organization that represents your area of work. Many of these publish rate-guidance information and can provide a good indicator.

2. **PUBLISHED OPPORTUNITIES** are all those job adverts and freelance callouts that you can find online in your sector. Don't worry if these are a little out of date, they will still have rates attached to them that you can use as a guide.

   When you are comparing *permanent* job opportunities, first check that the job is aimed at your level of experience. Then when you are looking at the salary remember that it costs an employer more than the salary offered to employ someone. They must provide all the tools for them to do the work (desk, computer, phone etc.), and in most jurisdictions employers have to pay a percentage of the employee's salary to the tax authority. A rough rule of thumb would be that the cost to a company of an employee is a further 25 per cent on top of advertised salary.

3. **ASKING PEOPLE** is the final area to benchmark. Freelancers all want to get paid a fair rate to do the work they do and will often be supportive of those looking to define their value. It's probably not the wisest move to

ask colleagues how much they are being paid, but you can play on their good nature. People like to help others, so see if you can identify anyone in your network likely to have good intelligence on your sector and then find a convenient moment to seek their advice. Explain that you are trying to work out your value and explain clearly what level you see yourself at before asking them what they think your value should be. If you consult several people you may well start to see a pattern. And you've also just advertised your services to all of them, which can't be bad.

INDUSTRY SECTOR VARIATIONS

There is one big caveat to your research so far. This information is specific to the segment of the industry you have been researching. If, like me, you use your knowledge and experience to deliver your services to a range of customers in different industries or sectors then you may need to expand your benchmarking accordingly. The value of your work for a client in one segment of the industry may not hold in another.

For example, if I am working as a TV production manager there are accepted rates I can charge for my time. But if I am using this same production management expertise to teach university students about what the job entails my TV rate is unlikely to apply; instead I will be paid a teaching rate that could be by the hour rather than by the day or the week.

Different industry segments can have markedly different rates for the same work. This goes back to your customer analysis of the type of clients you are looking to work with. A small charity is likely to pay less than a large corporate client, so if you are aiming to work with both you will have to quote different rates.

Don't worry, having a series of rates is fine. The challenge is to quote the right one to the right client, and the more informed you can be about the different areas you want to work in, the better you'll be able to achieve this.

Valuation analysis	Research	Estimated rate
What I need to earn to live	Valuation based on an estimated rate	
	Valuation based on number of working days in year	
Experience	My experience level is	
Benchmarking	Sector Resources research and info	
	Published Opportunities research and info	
	Asking people research and info	
Sector variations	I will be delivering my services in these sectors	
Intended audiences	Variations in intended audience are	

WHO IS YOUR INTENDED AUDIENCE?

Finally, even within a client or a segment your rate may vary depending on the intended audience for a piece of work. Something where the work your client is doing is speculative (such as design work needed for a pitch) may mean you are asked to work for a reduced rate, usually on the proviso that you would get the work should the full project come off. These can be great opportunities for you to deepen a relationship with a client by helping them out, but you need to watch out for the client who only hires you for pitch work that never comes off and doesn't give you any full-priced work.

Use the valuation analysis table on page 98 to pull together all your thinking about your rate and your value in the marketplace. As you review the table entries you should be building up a picture of the market and how you can value yourself. Finding your monetary value can be challenging, especially if it is in a new area for you.

Your true worth lies in how much you can make a client value your offer. When I buy a designer item, I know that the cost of producing the item is significantly less than the retail price, and that a large part of that mark-up is in the value I ascribe to owning it. The same principle applies here. As you value yourself and your services you should think about how you can move towards the designer end of the scale.

Consider the example of a freelancer who had a thriving business as a wedding photographer and was booked up a year in advance. As the summer is a peak period for getting married, and Saturday is the most popular day, she had probably around thirteen Saturdays in any year during which she did the majority of her work. She couldn't influence the marketplace to increase the number of these peak spots for weddings, but she could influence the price she charged.

She took a step back, assessed her value in the marketplace and decided to double her prices. The bookings came in just as before, so she put her prices up again. She could even turn down work if it wasn't in a location that suited her. By this stage she was earning more than double what she had been and was taking on more preferable bookings. She understood her value in the marketplace and used that knowledge to extract the maximum value for herself.

Now that you have an idea of where you might value yourself generally, let's look at some indicators that will help you conduct a more granular analysis.

OVERPRICING

Being offered insufficient work could indicate that you are overpricing. You have new client meetings and send in your proposal or your CV but you aren't converting this to paid work. Overpricing doesn't necessarily mean that you are charging too much; it could simply mean that the clients you are pitching to can't or won't pay what you are worth. Again, this goes back to the values discussion from earlier. Ask yourself if you are trying to attract clients who value your work in the same way that you do. It may be time to think about which clients you want to work with and how you can start to focus your efforts on getting work from those who will pay a proper rate for what you do (more on this in Chapter 9, 'Turning Your Contacts into Customers').

UNDERPRICING

Conversely, a key indicator that you've underpriced is that you are being offered too much work. You may think, 'That's great! I've got work coming out of my ears. I'll not go hungry now.' But there is such a thing as a busy fool and this is where you really need to know your value – it could be that a busload of work has come along at once as a normal part of the 'feast and famine' freelancing cycle. But it could also be that your clients see you as being cheap for the value you bring, and they all want a piece of you. You don't want to be that person.

If you are just starting out and trying to build a portfolio you might be tempted to use this 'too good value' strategy – but don't expect these clients to stay with you as you increase your prices.

They will move on swiftly to the next freelancer desperate for work. That doesn't mean that the strategy has no merit: you'll have gained experience by including that work in your portfolio and this can lead to you taking on bigger clients at higher rates.

Perhaps you are a graphic designer trying to attract a new client in an industry sector that you're keen to break into. You can absolutely offer them a deal at a lower rate, but you should stress this is an introductory offer, otherwise they may assume that you are always cheap and then it can prove problematic to get your full rate for the next piece of work.

Being considered cheap can also have a negative impact on the client's perception of the quality of your work. Think about it. When you go shopping, what is your perception of the cheapest items on the shelves? If you are anything like me then you think it is cheap for a reason, and that something must have been compromised along the way. That's not the impression you want to create.

A simple rule of thumb is that if you are too busy then, like the wedding photographer did, put your prices up. Yes, you will lose some clients, but as the other clients will be paying more you'll end up doing less work for the same reward.

This graph shows a simple relationship between price and demand for services. You earn the same overall along the line. However, as the price rises, demand falls so you do fewer hours for the same money. Reduce the price and demand will increase so you'll be doing more hours for the money. This model makes one big assumption that your

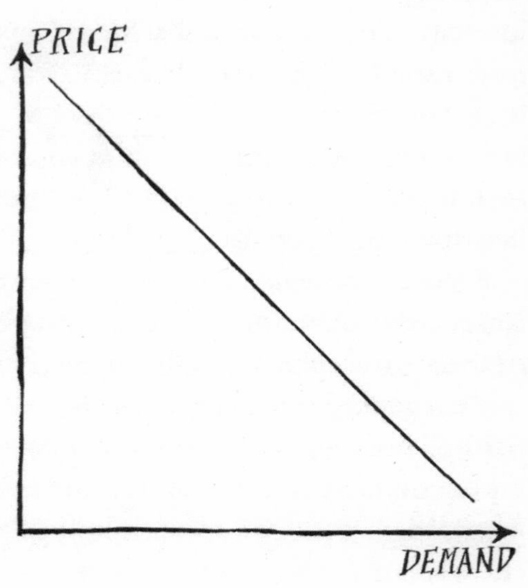

pricing is at the balance point in the market. In the wedding photographer example she was underpricing so even though she put her prices up demand stayed the same. It was only when she put them up further again that she saw the demand fall and knew that she had reached the balance point in her marketplace for her services.

You can use this knowledge to your advantage when you are considering how to price your services in relation to your competition. Just remember that the only winner in a price war is the customer. A price war creates a race to the bottom as everyone ends up trying to undercut everyone else.

When it comes to your competition, it is extremely useful to know how they are pricing similar work. You will be setting your own prices, but knowledge of who the competition is, what their experience is and how they are pricing is helpful. Remember as well that you cannot collude with competitors to inflate prices artificially. This will land you in court!

EXPLOITATION

Exploitation is a contentious word that primarily centres around low pay. The million-dollar questions are, when is working for free 'exploitation' and when is it 'valuable experience'? When is it acceptable to work more hours or days for a client than they are paying you to get the job done and when is it not? There are no one-size-fits-all answers to these questions – it really is a personal decision where you draw the line.

Financial exploitation isn't just something that happens only to freelancers who are starting out. It can happen to all freelancers regardless of their experience. The difference is in the way it presents itself.

Experienced freelancers find that clients will play on their good nature, and long after a project is completed come back and start asking supplementary questions or for information you've already provided. This can be a very murky area, especially if they are a client who's given you a lot of work. As a professional freelancer I try to be as helpful as I can to my clients as I know they value this. But when such a situation arises, as it does from time to time, I always ask myself whether what I'm being asked for is actually something that I should be paid extra to do. If so, then I'll usually point out that they are commissioning a piece of work, however big or small, and it will take me some time to complete, so I will need to charge for it.

Exploitation can also rear its head in the form of project creep, where the client starts to add in more and more elements to the brief that hadn't been discussed up front and will mean extra work for you at no extra cost to them. Again, this needs careful management so that it doesn't become exploitation through the back door. But it's never that simple. This is where a well-planned project with a detailed proposal clearly outlining what you will deliver for the client will stand you in good stead. If you've all agreed to that at the start then you have scope for negotiation on the extra elements now being asked for. (Again, there is more on this in Chapter 9, 'Turning Your Contacts into Customers'.)

WORKING FOR LOW PAY

If you are concerned because you are being paid low rates regularly then you need to look hard at why this is the case. Perhaps you now have the experience to command a higher rate. If so, ask yourself why you aren't being offered it. The most common answer I hear is either 'I haven't asked' or 'I don't think my clients can afford it'. This shows a lack of confidence in the value they bring to the table for the services they deliver, and an inability to articulate this.

Perhaps you are in a cycle of exploitation – your clients won't pay a higher hourly or daily rate for your work and it often takes longer than you expected. Think about how you can break out of this vicious circle. It's probably time to reassess whether your clients are good customers.

Hand in hand with this cycle is the fear of losing work if you charge higher rates. Whilst this can be a very real concern, I have found that, when pushed, freelancers in this situation are more focussed on how the client values them rather than how they value the client. As you develop and grow you will inevitably change your clientele. Clients who were good or even great when you were starting out may not have the need for your more experienced services (or be willing to pay for them), so you will need to move on and find new clients who value both your offering and your level of experience.

WORKING FOR NOTHING

If you are just starting out there can be valid short-term reasons why you might offer clients some low-paid or unpaid work to build up your portfolio, but it's a fine line between building your portfolio and being exploited.

You need a very good reason to work for nothing, and you need to be clear in your head why you are happy to do this and how long you are prepared to do it for. Some industries, especially the creative, have a reputation for expecting people to work for nothing, so be sure if you do plan to offer free work at any time you know what you are getting into.

Rather than think of it as working for nothing, think about the reason you are taking this work on. It must have **real** value to you – even if it is not monetary – so in effect there is a transaction taking place.

If you are starting out as a graphic designer then you will want to have a portfolio to show prospective clients, in which case you might offer to do some *pro bono* work in a limited capacity. Just make sure the clients to whom you are offering any free work will give you real value in return.

The key to making this pay off for you (pardon the pun) is to be clear in your mind about your boundaries to working for no fee. Be clear with yourself about how much time you are prepared to invest (or, more realistically, can invest) in no-fee work, why you are taking this particular opportunity and what you expect to gain from it. Be strategic.

In addition – and in my experience this is where most people fail – make sure the client you are doing the no-fee work for is clear about why you are doing this for free and exactly what you will do. I'm not suggesting laying down a set of demands, just ensuring that in the discussions you have with the client they appreciate the value you are bringing and why you are prepared to waive payment.

It could be that you're happy to do a job for no fee to gain experience and credibility in a particular sector. If that's the case, you will want to be able to shout about how you've worked for the client, so make sure you *can* shout about it before committing to doing the work. It's absolutely right and proper that you ask for testimonials and potentially even recommendations in return for your time. Just make sure both your and the client's expectations are made clear up front.

THE HOBBY CLIENT

If you have a client who genuinely can't pay your full rate then you need to consider whether they are a client you want to work with for the longer term. There may be non-financial reasons to do so, such as caring passionately about what it is they do. If that is the case then think of working for them as a hobby. Working with hobby clients is a way you can use your expertise to good effect in supporting a cause you believe in. Just don't get this type of work confused with work that will allow you to live the life you described in your living budget. It will not pay the bills and shouldn't be included in your working-time calculations on page 88. The reason you are helping out is that you believe in what you're doing and want to make a difference, but it isn't work per se.

Finally, if ever you are the victim of financial exploitation, don't forget it is your right simply to walk away as soon as the current contract is completed, and never work for them again.

KNOWING WHEN TO TURN DOWN WORK

Turning down offers of low-paid work is a tough call because there's always that nagging fear that nothing will come along to fill the gap. Your confidence starts to take a knock as you begin to think no one will pay your true rates. But if you keep thinking like that and taking on work at low-ball rates, you'll end up being really busy. And really poor.

And it gets worse; it's amazing how quickly word gets round when good people undervalue themselves, so you will become overwhelmed with offers, leaving you no time to work *on* your business and develop better clients who will value your services properly. This is a vicious circle and breaking out of it is difficult.

As you gain experience and start to increase your rates you may find that some clients don't grow with you. You will then have a choice; do you continue working for them at the lower rate or do you move on?

If they are good customers, you might allow them some leeway. Think about how much work they give you, how time consuming it is and whether they are a good source of referrals. Perhaps their brand is very strong and it's important for you to stay associated with them. Otherwise, this may be a good time to look for new business.

Only you can be the judge of where on the scale each client sits. If you do want to move on, be sure to part on amicable terms. Do the good-freelancer deed and recommend someone who could take over the work you've been doing for them rather than leaving them with a problem to solve.

HOW DO I PUT MY PRICES UP?

The simple answer is tell your clients you are going to do this and then do it. The client will either agree or not. You need to have decided beforehand what you will do if they reject your price rise: walk away or carry on as usual. Be aware that carrying on as usual after asking for a price rise is likely to be the beginning of the end of your relationship, as you will feel increasingly undervalued, especially when your other clients have agreed to the increase.

MODELS OF CHARGING FOR WORK

You can be hired in a variety of ways but, with a few exceptions, you will usually be paid at an hourly, daily or weekly rate, or given a price for the whole project.

BY THE HOUR

Working by the hour might be done by freelancers such as graphic designers and virtual assistants. They will generally have many clients who, in an ideal world, will provide regular repeat business or retain them for a guaranteed number of hours per month.

BY THE DAY

Work booked by the day might be offered to freelancers such as film crews or workshop facilitators. They too will usually have a large number of clients and, again, they will want to be building long-term relationships with the aim of securing regular work and, ideally, whole-project bookings.

If you are offered a day rate, it's important to define what a 'day' means – I've done day-long jobs that have lasted anything from six to sixteen hours.

BY THE WEEK

Bookings by the week might include TV production work or planning an event. The agreement for this type of work is often described as a short-term fixed contract. Clients are likely to insist upon your working exclusively for them during the contracted period. You may also find that, although you have a five-day-per-week contract of say

37.5 hours per week, there is no overtime provision so any additional hours worked will be at no extra pay.

Even though the contract is full time, because it is for a fixed period, your mindset should remain firmly that of a freelancer. You're hired to fill a full-time position for a finite span. Remember, at the end of the contract, the job is complete and you will be the person finding new work for you to do.

BY THE PROJECT

Work booked by the project often comprises a package of days to be completed during a specific period. A marketing consultant, for instance, might be hired to carry out research to a brief by a client who will offer fifteen days' work over a period of two months. It will be up to them to schedule the work necessary, including any meetings and/or report writing, in the required time.

Alternatively, you might be offered a fixed sum to complete a project to a given deadline. You will need to consider how long the job is likely to take, and therefore how much you will earn per hour or per day. Be careful! If you make a mistake here you could find yourself working for too little if you underestimate the time it will take, or turning down a lucrative commission if you overestimate it.

It's worth being aware of the implications of exclusivity when you are discussing terms with a client on project work; it's unwise to agree to anything that precludes you from earning a living with other similar clients.

OVERTIME

Overtime means working more hours than you are contracted for, and it can apply just as much to freelancing as to paid employment. It is usually associated with daily or weekly bookings and is particularly prevalent in unionized sectors where long days are the norm. Film crews are a good example. Filming is always the 'big money' day, so you can expect it to last at least ten hours and sometimes even fourteen or more. Film crews will often quote for a ten-hour day, with the first two hours' overtime at that same hourly rate and anything over twelve hours at time and a half.

Consider whether you want to build in a provision for overtime in the agreements you reach with clients.

SHOW ME THE MONEY!

You need to consider all of the factors discussed when talking to potential and existing clients so that you can price your time accordingly.

Equally important is understanding where you add value to your clients and the 'special sauce' you bring that makes them want to work with you. Many people think it is because they have X experience or Y clients, but if you talk to their clients it's always more than that – professional communications and organization count for an awful lot. So does a sense of humour.

Now put all your thinking together and see if the numbers will work for you. Do you think you have one rate or several? If several rates, then estimate the percentage of work done at each rate over a year, as in the examples below.

EXAMPLE 1: DAILY RATE VARIATION

A freelance workshop facilitator is booked by the day and plans to work 120 days per year. They also have a high level of outgoings for the year.

	Daily rate	% of work	Working days per annum (est. 120)	Annual earnings
Rate 1	500	20	24	12,000
Rate 2	250	50	60	15,000
Rate 3	300	30	36	10,800
Projected turnover				37,800
Required turnover				40,000
REALITY CHECK: shortfall or excess				-2,200

This example shows that their projected turnover for the year doesn't reach the level of their expected outgoings (required turnover). However, their estimate for paid days worked in the year is low, so a small increase in number of paid days will balance this out – an additional eight days' work at their middle rate, for instance, would make the numbers add up.

EXAMPLE 2: WEEKLY RATE VARIATION

A social-media assistant is booked by the week and plans to work thirty-six paid weeks per year. Whilst their outgoings are lower than in the previous example, they too are finely balanced in making the numbers work.

	Weekly rate	% of work	Working weeks per annum (est. 36)	Annual earnings
Rate 1	500	33.3	12	6,000
Rate 2	400	33.3	12	4,800
Rate 3	600	33.3	12	7,200
Projected turnover				18,000
Required turnover				17,500
REALITY CHECK: shortfall or excess				+500

This example shows that working thirty-six weeks of the year leaves them with an estimated additional week's money, but that could easily change if more of their work was at the lowest rate. Additionally, whilst thirty-six weeks per year sounds as though it leaves plenty to spare, as there are fifty-two weeks in a year, it's surprising how quickly the available weeks to work decrease.

Most people take two weeks off at Christmas and a week at Easter, plus a two-week summer break. That's already five weeks unpaid – taking your maximum down to forty-seven. And then if you have eight short contracts over the year and following each you find you have a week's gap due to project timings, you're down to thirty-nine weeks of potential paid working in the year. You can see quickly why estimating that you will work forty-eight paid weeks per year is not realistic.

Work out your own reality check in the blank table provided. You might want to do a couple of versions based on lower and higher numbers of working days or weeks to see where your break-even point is. Use the turnover figure you calculated on page 88 to assist you.

	Rate/____	% of work	Working weeks/year (est. ____)	Est. earnings p.a.
Rate 1				
Rate 2				
Rate 3				
Projected turnover				
Required turnover				
REALITY CHECK: shortfall or excess				

This is your reality check on the viability of your freelance working as you currently see it, based on how much you estimate you will work per year, the rate you think you can charge and how that maps with your personal situation and your estimated outgoings.

If they are working for you then you can crack on with articulating your vision in the next chapter. If, however, it doesn't look like you can break even then it's important to figure out why and how you might fix it. Ultimately, if the numbers say that you will spend more than you will earn, you will need to find a way to spend less or earn more. Look at the calculations you made here and in Chapter 4 and see if you can make any adjustments to your estimates and analyses before moving on.

Your reality check should be ongoing. If your financial situation changes at any point, the first thing you should always do is re-examine the numbers in the light of those changes.

6.

ARTICULATING YOUR VISION

This chapter will explore how you articulate both your *visual* and *verbal* brand identity. ***You are your brand*** – **'Brand Me'**. Your ***values*** are what you are selling as well as your ***expertise***.

Now, it's time to decide if you will use your own name or a company name for your services. There are no rights or wrongs about which is best. Much will depend on the sectors you will be working in.

Some public-sector bodies prefer to work with companies rather than individuals, so giving yourself a company name, even if you are operating solo, can offer you flexibility. The flipside of this is that you are selling yourself and your services, so operating under your own name has its benefits too. Another consideration is that, if you want to grow and take on others to work with you, packaging yourself as a company rather than as a personal brand might be preferable. Make your decision.

From now on Brand Me is known as:

. . . .

I expect you already have a vision of what your brand looks like, but now it's time to start using the values you identified earlier (go back to Chapter 2 to remind yourself if you need to) in order to properly package and articulate 'Brand Me'.

You need to do this *before* you start looking for customers; imagine you're in front of your first potential client and they ask, 'Why should I choose you?' You need to have a sincere and compelling answer that's relevant to them. It needs to be tailored to each client, so a contrived sales-speak 'standard' answer just won't cut it.

This is where your values come in: they provide the building blocks for all your communications wherever and whenever you are communicating the message about why your customers should choose you. The great thing is, they can be applied to pretty much everything:

✓ Website
✓ Mission statement
✓ Pitches
✓ Presentations
✓ Client emails
✓ Client meetings

Not only will this simplify your life because you have a bank of words, phrases, sentences and paragraphs that you can use time and time again, it will also improve the clarity and consistency of your communications.

First, it's time for a bit more marketing theory to help you to focus these communications for your different types of customers.

SEGMENTATION, TARGETING, POSITIONING

You organize the market research you've done through the funnel of segmentation, targeting and positioning (STP). For this you need to go back to the research you did on customers in Chapter 3.

Unlike the 3Cs analysis – which can be done in any order – STP needs to be done in sequence:

- **Segmentation** is where you divide your customers (or potential customers) into different groups or segments.
- **Targeting** is the act of prioritizing which segments you target.
- **Positioning** is how you make your service appealing to your customer segment.

SEGMENTATION

Segmentation divides your customers into groups or types. The goal is to identify segments that need different benefits or values from your offering. A bit like client-focussed thinking, you have to *identify customers' needs* and segment them into groups with *similar needs*. Look back at your customer analysis and identify your different *types* of customers. There are two basic ways to start your segmentation – by business type or by service.

For businesses you can look at characteristics such as size, location, how long they've been established, their financial situation and/or their industry sector. For example, you could start by looking at which firms are on your doorstep and might value your services. You might prefer to work with a certain size of company or have a specific service you offer to smaller companies and a different service to larger companies.

If these factors don't feel relevant, then perhaps company culture might be more appropriate. It might be better to segment your customers by their level of innovation, their business sophistication, their growth aims or their level of technology usage.

In the space provided, start by filling in the first column with all the customer segments you've identified. For example: a digital media expert might actively seek out companies who could use more technology to drive growth so they would segment companies by their level of technology use.

An alternative method for segmentation is to look at service-related characteristics. What I mean by this is looking at how a

My customer segments are	Already working with? (Y/N)	Target no.	Priority (short/med/ long term)

company might *make use* of your services, *how much* of them they might need at any one time, *how frequently* they purchase your services and who the *users* of your services are. For example, a graphic designer might be able to segment customers into those who utilize their services occasionally and those who are regular users.

As an expert in your field you will need to examine your existing customers and the ones you want to attract, then think about how best you can segment them in the way that makes the most sense to *you*.

Remember that if you have a portfolio career with distinct strands you will want to consider each strand as a *different business* for marketing purposes, which means that you will need to do bespoke market research and prepare an individual marketing plan for each strand.

When I do this exercise to look at my portfolio of work, I find it easiest to first break down the types of work I do and then look at the different customer segments I can offer these to. It very quickly starts to look like a family tree with me at the top, the portfolio of services I offer on the next row, and below that the different customer segments that each aspect of my portfolio targets.

Sometimes the same customer segment appears in more than one place. This is fine. It just means you have two or more potential bites at that particular cherry.

The key aim of segmenting is to end up with a list of segments that you can readily identify and that are *self-identifying* (i.e. your customers would categorize themselves as being in these segments). Be clear which segments you are already working with, then add others you aspire to be working with.

Once you have this in place you are ready to move on to targeting.

TARGETING

Targeting is one of my favourite aspects of putting a marketing plan together. It's a pivotal point where you start to transition from the market-research phase to actually choosing the customer segments you will focus your efforts on.

You have your list of customer segments. Now you need to prioritize them into a targeting list. Think about which segments you are uniquely placed to service and those whose needs you can service better than your competition. A key principle I stick to is 'greed, with prudence', by which I mean identify those segments that have money to spend and are active in your area, possibly serving larger or expanding markets, and look for the low-hanging fruit: opportunities to use your networks or experience to make the maximum impact most quickly.

Number the list of customer segments you just made according to their importance to you. Targeting should also identify short-, medium- and long-term customers or opportunities so fill these in as well.

And that's it.

If you have a portfolio career this is also the time to prioritize which *strand* of work you will focus on, or you will struggle with the sheer volume of actively marketing all aspects of your work simultaneously.

POSITIONING

Positioning is the last step in the market research phase. It is where you put your inner spin doctor to work devising how you are going to position your services to appeal to the customer segments you've targeted. Each customer segment will require its own separate positioning activity, so bear this in mind when considering how many customer segments you can realistically target at any one time.

Marketing textbooks break down a positioning statement into a sequence of 'positioning elements'. This is a way of helping you concentrate on why a customer should value your services. Your positioning statement frames the conversation in terms of how the customer perceives you and your industry, then explains why what you do is different/better/faster and, finally, provides evidence. It's the spin you use naturally, broken down into a template so you can hone it and make it even better (see figure). You will and do know the answers to fill in the blanks, so let's break it down.

To ______________________________

<Target Customer Segment>

______________________________,

<Brand Me>

Is the brand of ______________________________

<Frame of Reference (FOR): Product/Service category as perceived by target customer>

that is ______________________________

<Point of Differentiation (POD): Basis of differentiation from other products/services in the target customer's FOR>,

Because ______________________________

<Rationale: Evidence provided to target customer to believe the FOR and POD>

- **Target Customer Segment** – This is the first customer segment you are targeting, and you already know this so fill it in.

- **Brand Me** – This is the name of your service.
- **Frame of Reference** (FOR) – This is the product or service category that you operate in as perceived by your target customer. Remember, you need to think about how your customer sees the world and where they might place you. This can often be different from where you see yourself.
- **Point of Differentiation** (POD) – This is the basis on which your services differ from other product or service offerings within your customer segment's frame of reference. Again, remember to look at this through the lens of your target customer segment.
- **Rationale** – This is the evidence you provide to your target customer segment to help them believe the FOR and the POD.

I have included here the positioning statement I put together when I was building up Girls Angels. The company was based in Central London and our primary customer segment was women working in Central London.

To Professional working women in Central London,
<Target Customer Segment>

Girls Angels ,
<Brand Me>

Is the brand of motorbike training school,
<Frame of Reference (FOR): Product/Service category as perceived by target customer>

that is most female friendly
<Point of Differentiation (POD): Basis of differentiation from other products/services in the target customer's FOR>,

Because we understand how women need to learn to ride a motorbike
<Rationale: Evidence provided to target customer to believe the FOR and POD>

Now it's time to get your inner spin doctor working and write your positioning statements for each of your target customer segments. If you have quite a few segments, start by writing the positioning statements for the first four on your target list. This will give

MY POSITIONING STATEMENTS:

To ____________________
<Target Customer Segment>

____________________,
<Brand Me>

Is the brand of ____________________
<Frame of Reference (FOR): Product/Service category as perceived by target customer>

that is ____________________
<Point of Differentiation (POD): Basis of differentiation from other products/services in the target customer's FOR>,

Because ____________________
<Rationale: Evidence provided to target customer to believe the FOR and POD>

To ____________________
<Target Customer Segment>

____________________,
<Brand Me>

Is the brand of ____________________
<Frame of Reference (FOR): Product/Service category as perceived by target customer>

that is ____________________
<Point of Differentiation (POD): Basis of differentiation from other products/services in the target customer's FOR>,

Because ____________________
<Rationale: Evidence provided to target customer to believe the FOR and POD>

To ____________________
<Target Customer Segment>

____________________,
<Brand Me>

Is the brand of ____________________
<Frame of Reference (FOR): Product/Service category as perceived by target customer>

that is ____________________
<Point of Differentiation (POD): Basis of differentiation from other products/services in the target customer's FOR>,

Because ____________________
<Rationale: Evidence provided to target customer to believe the FOR and POD>

To ____________________
<Target Customer Segment>

____________________,
<Brand Me>

Is the brand of ____________________
<Frame of Reference (FOR): Product/Service category as perceived by target customer>

that is ____________________
<Point of Differentiation (POD): Basis of differentiation from other products/services in the target customer's FOR>,

Because ____________________
<Rationale: Evidence provided to target customer to believe the FOR and POD>

you practice and help you articulate the subtly different ways you talk to your customer segments.

If your positioning statements are reading the same, then stop! Either you haven't quite got to grips with positioning or you might have separated two customer segments you didn't need to.

SUMMARY STP

Segmentation, targeting and positioning completes your market research.

You have **segmented** your **potential customers** into **groups**, prioritized whom you are going to **target** and written your **positioning statement** for each.

You should now see that prioritizing your target customer segments is vital to enable you to focus your marketing efforts, particularly if you have a portfolio career.

It's now time to move on to the active part of your marketing plan and put all this research and analysis into action. You do this with your *marketing mix*.

THE MARKETING MIX

The 'marketing mix' is how you pull together all your market research and articulate your offer to a potential customer. There are four elements in the mix, known as the 4Ps. Think of them as four ingredients which you can vary in quantity to find the right mix for each customer segment.

- **Product** or service offering – what are you selling?
- **Price** – how much for?
- **Promotion** – how will you talk to the customer?
- **Place** (or distribution) – sold where?

It's likely you'll have a range of services you can offer to clients. Now you need to review what it is you're selling but *looking through the lens of your target customer segments*.

And just like in the positioning exercise, in order to market effectively to each separate customer segment, you will need to look at them separately and to put together a bespoke marketing mix for each. The first three Ps are considered below. The fourth warrants a chapter of its own.

PRODUCT (OR SERVICE)

Let's start with the product, or more likely service you will be offering to a potential customer segment, and let's look at it from that customer segment's perspective. I find it helps to visualize a potential customer from that segment and then think about what parts of your service would add the most value for them, what you can improve and whom you are competing against.

A simple SWOT analysis helps here (see page 122). This time it is focussed on the **one service** you are offering to **one specific customer segment**.

Think about the distinctive features and benefits you bring. Just as in the skills audit you looked at yourself as a whole, do the same here. What is it about you and your specific skillset that is unique to you? This can often be the real difference in why you get work and others don't when you have similar skillsets.

If you can express what you offer in terms of the features and benefits, then you can explain why it is superior. For example: 'I offer [this service] to you the customer and that means . . .'

The words *and that means* are really simple and useful. They are a great selling tool. It allows you to link *features* of what you offer with a *customer benefit*. Think about your interactions with your customers to date. I know many freelancers who offer bespoke services find that they can get stuck in circular conversations with potential clients.

Customer Segment:	
Strengths What do I do well? Does my service perform the way my customer wants?	**Weaknesses** What can I improve?
Opportunities How do I grow this customer segment? Why me?	**Threats** What is my competition doing? Why not me?

When I was producing web films for companies my clients would regularly ask how much a film would cost. Anyone who's ever made a film before will roll their eyes and laugh at this – the client might as well be asking how long is a piece of string. But what it showed me was that I wasn't talking the same language as them and I needed to change the way I presented my services so that it was clear what the outcomes would be for the client at various price points.

So I took our filmmaking services and I 'productized' them. I created what I called Bronze, Silver and Gold templates for our services. With each template I made assumptions about how many days would be spent prepping, filming and editing, and therefore roughly how long a film they might be able to achieve, and then

I worked out what each templated 'product' cost. I planned them to span a range of price points that would allow me to identify quickly what sort of spend a client had in mind.

I now had a tool for when I was with clients to say in response to that question, 'Well, to get a film like this you need this much filming, that much editing and so on, which will cost this much.' I made sure I retained a bespoke element by saying this was an example, but that if they gave me a bit more detail, I could provide a more accurate cost based on their precise needs. What I had done was to translate the job into a packaged 'product' that helped the customer understand what they could get for their money. It had the added benefit of helping me ascertain what sort of budget the client had in mind, as they would home in on either the Gold, Silver or Bronze product as the conversation evolved.

The productization of our filmmaking services allowed me to articulate our vision and break free of the circular conversation with clients so that we could move forward and identify quickly and easily what they might be looking for.

It's not just filmmaking in which 'productization' can be effective. It works well for *any* freelancer who provides bespoke services for clients. I've seen the light come on with graphic designers and event planners when I've used this tool in workshops.

Now that you've looked in more detail at your service offering for your target customer segment you should start to feel a sense of confidence about how you can articulate your vision and engage a potential new customer. Don't forget that you've only looked at one of your customer segments so far; you'll need to repeat this exercise for every target customer segment and service you offer.

PRICE

It may come as a surprise to you that pricing is an ingredient in the marketing mix – but pricing is a very valuable weapon *when used strategically*.

So far, you've looked at what you need to earn to live and estimated what your value should be in the marketplace. Your price *within the marketing mix* is where you determine what you will charge for each service you offer to each customer segment. It's also about how you handle a price conversation. As you've seen already, changing the price can affect the demand for your services. It also signals the value you attach to the service you are offering.

Cheapness is not a virtue. Nor is it a product or service feature.

Let's think about this for a moment. You are busy. You have work coming out of your ears. 'Wonderful!' you think. 'I'm really in demand.' But is it really so great? It could be that the marketplace has realized that you are doing a cracking job and not charging properly for it. Remember the example of the wedding photographer who put up her prices. Think about how this could apply to you. If you're really busy, try putting up your prices and see what happens.

Be shrewd about how you use pricing. Use it as a tool to manage your workload and take on the jobs you want to do. Make the trickier clients pay more. You won't mind their trickiness so much then.

That said, when it comes to pricing the best conversations with clients are those you have when you are not talking about price at all. The best conversations are focussed entirely on how you can work together and how you can solve their current problems, rather than what it will cost them. Also, when you're having that sort of conversation it's a 'buying signal' – chances are they've already bought in to Brand You and you can stop selling yourself. There's more on buying signals in Chapter 9, 'Turning Your Contacts into Customers'.

NOT TALKING ABOUT PRICE

This may sound like an impossible dream. You are selling your services. How can you sell them without talking about price? Surely price is the only thing the customer is interested in?

I beg to differ; the customer is interested in developing their business. They will buy in services that solve their problems and that meet their aims and objectives. Of course, there is a limit to what they will pay for them. Your job is to talk their language and help them understand how much value you can add to their business by doing the work you do, thereby selling to them on the *value* of your services.

This subject came up in very sharp focus on one particular training course I ran. The participants talked about how their customers brought up price straight away in their conversations as they were very price sensitive. Their sales conversations solely revolved around price and the level of discount they could offer. They felt there was no way to navigate this conversation away from price and that they just had to bite the bullet and negotiate.

Then, I challenged the group to think about reasons why their product or service was so good and what a difference it would make to their price-sensitive client. I asked them, 'What value could it add to your client to buy your products or services?'

The participants all started to come up with reasons that their product or service was valuable and essential to the client that didn't include price. They all had answers to the question. So they could now engage with a client about the value they added – and steer the conversation away from price.

You want to aim to have **all** your clients biting your hand off for your services before you even discuss price. When you can do this, talking about money becomes a practicality and function of delivering the work rather than that moment of terror that you are on an inevitable crash course towards during your entire pitch.

THE SHARP-INTAKE-OF-BREATH TEST

I love the 'sharp-intake-of-breath' test when setting pricing. It's simple, easy to implement and very effective. When a client asks you how much the job you are discussing will cost and you **don't** hear a sharp intake of breath when you tell them, then you've underpriced yourself. Remember, your work has a value – and you want to ensure it is valued highly by your clients.

Think about it – when something is priced high and at the top end of your expectations you believe it to be better than something priced lower. That's the end of the scale you want to be at. So, listen out for that sharp intake of breath and learn to love it.

A classic example of this is buying a car. There is a deal to be done when you're buying a car. You know what situation you are walking into. You might be in a car showroom and the salesperson is showing you a vehicle you like the look of. The price is usually displayed on the windscreen so you can't miss it. You've probably done your research about what you are after, how much it should cost etc. You know the salesperson's role – not only are they there to sell cars, they want to sell them at the highest price they can. So, it's all a game. You make an offer, they counter it, and so on until, hopefully, you agree a deal. At the end you both want to feel like you have secured a bargain. But consider what happens if you make that initial offer and the salesperson just accepts it. Think about how that would make you feel. You are likely to wonder why the salesperson didn't try to extract more value from you in the negotiation. Don't be the freelancer who gives away too much value by selling yourself too low, so that your clients never negotiate with you.

If you have priced at the sharp-intake-of-breath level then there is potentially a little room for negotiation between you and your client in a way that will still leave you in pocket and happy with the outcome. If you've offered a low rate to a client and they still do the sharp intake of breath, you might want to question how good a customer they really are.

Britons tend to like a negotiation outcome where everyone gets a good deal, but it's not the same everywhere so you must do your research if selling to a different audience. Some cultures are averse to bargaining whilst for others it's a vital part of the mix; some negotiate aggressively but to others this is anathema because harmony is more important. The list goes on.

Personally, I love to hear that sharp intake of breath when I propose a rate. It means I've pitched it at the right level. A quick agreement without a negotiation or hesitation always makes me think I could have extracted more value from the situation.

WALK-AWAY PRICE

In any conversation with a client about pricing you need to be clear in your mind before you start the conversation what your 'walk-away' price will be – the price at which you walk away from the opportunity. These can be at different levels for different clients, but you never want to find that you've agreed a price lower than you can afford to take the work on at. It's easy to become swept up in the excitement of agreeing a proposal with a client and getting talked into something in the heat of the moment that you'll later regret.

Knowing your walk-away price from the outset will stand you in good stead because you know how far you will negotiate on price before saying no. And no can be very hard to say, particularly when you are not that busy.

In summary, it's not enough just to know what level you should be pricing your services at; you need to understand the signals you are giving and receiving when you talk about pricing and how to present your pricing to clients. All of these strategies will help you extract the maximum value from your clients for the work you do.

PROMOTION

Promotion is the third P in the marketing mix. Promotional activities are the communication efforts of your marketing plan. It's the part of the marketing plan where you begin to articulate your vision for each customer segment. Promotional activities are the stories you tell to communicate your offer.

There are many different promotional activities available. It's unlikely that you will take out a TV ad campaign, for example, but you could easily have a show reel or links to clips of you and your work on YouTube and on your website. It's up to you to consider which are the most relevant activities for promoting your services.

Your customers are buying **you** and therefore your promotional activities need to articulate clearly **why they should choose you**. You've done a lot of the thinking for this work already with the 3Cs analysis, your values and your positioning statements, and now it's time to put all this to work.

The best place to start with preparing your promotional materials is with the big picture and then drill down into more detail, which can then become more targeted to individual customer segments. If you are planning a portfolio offering then you will need to do this for each part of your offer.

MISSION STATEMENT

Your starting point is your mission statement. A short sentence that explains *Why Me?* If 'mission statement' doesn't sound quite right you could call it your key skill or core competency. Whatever you call it, devise a short sentence that reflects your offer and encompasses some or all of your brand values. This is exceptionally useful when you meet potential new clients as it allows you to say succinctly how the work you do can benefit their business.

For many years in my work with creative entrepreneurs I have used this:

Key skill – transforming creative concepts into a business reality

By calling it a key skill I have made this a more practically focussed mission statement – but then that's the business I'm in; practical support for freelancers and entrepreneurs looking to move their businesses forward.

For you, your mission statement should quickly allow people who don't know you to understand what you can do for them. Take a look back now at what you've written down previously about Why me? and Building Brand Me (pages 75 and 41) and take some time to prepare your own mission statement for your freelance work.

My mission statement:

Once you have your mission statement you can build on this to become a full pitch.

PITCH

A good pitch is one that is client-focussed, clear and concise.

Think back to people you've met who weren't necessarily the most talented in terms of the work they wanted to do but somehow always got the best opportunities. You've probably wondered why they were picked in preference to others you viewed as far more talented, possibly including yourself. It's probably because they knew instinctively how to pitch themselves at meetings and interviews. They knew how to talk to future employers or clients and particularly how to sell the benefits of themselves. Success is as much about approach and personality as it is experience – so make sure you aren't missing a trick and work on your pitching.

Just as with your different positioning statements, you will find you have different pitches for different customer segments as they'll have different needs and will value different aspects of your work. Once you've articulated your different pitches you can use them to form the basis of your marketing copy. It is important to be consistent in your messaging.

The following is a great framework for preparing your pitch.

- Headline
- Where's the pain?
- Solution
- People
- Results
- Ask

A good pitch covers each of these and should take no more than one minute to deliver. It also takes practice. Practise it by yourself and on your friends; then, and only then, move on to clients.

ARTICULATING YOUR VISION

In order to articulate your vision you will need to prepare your marketing materials, including:

- biography;
- website;
- blog;
- presentations and proposals;
- business cards;
- . . . anything else that you might want to prepare.

You might not need all of these, but you need to work out what is relevant to you and your work and prepare accordingly.

Within each of these marketing materials you will have some elements that are static and won't change and some that change

Headline	Open with the headline – an interesting fact about your business and what you do in an attention-grabbing way. Think of it as your tabloid newspaper headline
Where's the pain?	Explain the problem that the customer has
Solution	Explain the solution you propose
People	Who are you and what is your experience?
Results	Key facts about your success stories to date
Ask	What are you looking for from the person receiving the pitch?

or need updating regularly. Think about proposals you prepare for clients; some of them will be boilerplate copy that is the same for each proposal and some will be specific to that client. The same will be true of your website. There will be static content and there will be news and articles that you will want to update regularly.

As you begin to articulate your vision, start with the boilerplate copy that rarely changes. It is, in essence, your mission statement and your pitch written down in an eloquent and easy to understand way that is client-focussed. This copy will form the basis of your homepage and your proposals. As you write, keep asking yourself, 'Am I writing about *why* or have I strayed into *what*?' The notes you made about Why me? will form the basis of this copy.

Another important asset for your boilerplate copy is your professional biography.

BIOGRAPHY

Your professional biography is the carefully worded story of your working life. It should be written in such a way as to present you in the best light without sounding cocky. It should articulate the key strengths and experience you have. It should show a splash of personality and it should come across as confident.

To go with your biography, you will need a photograph of yourself, usually a headshot. Your photo needs to make you look suited to the industry you work in so dress appropriately. You'll look out of place if you don't and clients might think you don't understand their business.

Take some time now to write your biography. You will need it frequently. It shouldn't be more than a page, ideally closer to half a page. I have three versions of mine, a generic one, a sector specific one and a very short version.

Now that you have your pitch, boilerplate copy and biography you can put this to work on your marketing materials – starting with your website.

WEBSITE

Having a website is pretty much obligatory nowadays, but it doesn't have to be complicated and, in many ways, keeping it simple and inviting customers to get in touch can bring the best results; what you really want your website to do is make the phone ring or the emails ping. Once people have made contact you can start selling your services to them. Your site can, and should, evolve with you as your services develop.

Think of your website as a digital brochure designed for your audience – it showcases and sells your product or service, but a good brochure also leaves readers with questions they want answered.

Whilst it doesn't need to be complicated it does need to be *responsive* – set up to look good and render properly across a range of devices. A potential customer's first interaction with your site is as likely to be on a phone or tablet as on a PC or laptop, which is why search engines favour responsive sites. Most off-the-shelf web templates, design/hosting packages or themes are set up to do that out of the box nowadays, but make sure you check.

Site navigation should be simple and straightforward; if your client cannot find their way round your site intuitively, it is too complicated.

A classic example of this was the story of a company in the early 2000s at the height of the dotcom boom. They made a huge tech play by building a massively complicated website for online retailing of clothes. One day their website went down and they were forced to put up a holding page requesting customers call their sales line to make their purchases. That day – when their customers spoke to a person – they sold more than on any previous single day's trading.

A simple website should cover these basics:

- **Home page** – effectively, your pitch.
- **About you** – your biography and a professional picture.
- **Your services** – what you are selling dressed up as customer solutions.

- **Imagery** – pictures that illustrate what you can do.
- **Testimonials** – what your clients say about you.
- **Contact details** – how to connect with you and your social media.

The great news is you've done the first three and you should know your own contact details so this just leaves imagery and testimonials.

As well as words for your website, you'll need to find a selection of pictures that depict the work you do. If these are of work you have done for identifiable clients, you'll need to ensure that you have their permission to use them. If you don't have enough images of your own, perhaps clients will have something suitable that they would be happy for you to use. Failing that, if you are still in need of visuals there are a number of websites that provide royalty-free stock images for the web.

Testimonials are a very powerful tool. Put yourself in the shoes of a potential customer: who do you attach the most credibility to? Self-promotion or third-party recommendation? It's just like reading newspapers: you can easily tell the difference between editorial and advertising. Testimonials are your website's editorial.

So, reach out to some clients who can give you testimonials. If you are just starting out and haven't got a client list, then identify professionals you've worked with, studied under or who've mentored you and who can recommend you and your services.

As you consider who to approach, think about the companies you've worked with who will be the most impressive to potential clients. Once you've identified them, consider what they might want to say about you. To make it easy for them, it's not uncommon to enclose a draft testimonial with your request and send it over for them to tweak; that way you can be strategic and ensure your testimonials promote areas you want endorsed.

The people I will contact for testimonials are:

Name	Company	What they might want to say about me

The final details you need to put together are your contact details. It's vital you can be contacted easily, otherwise it's game over straight away. You'll want to consider the most appropriate communication channels for your type of work.

A contact form on your website that lands in your email is a must. A phone number is preferable as well. It will depend on the sector and type of work you do whether a mobile number alone will suffice or whether you prefer to offer a landline option. You also want to link to your social media channels so visitors to your website can easily join your conversation.

After all this work, when people do get in touch, be it via phone, email or social media, *make sure you respond promptly* and with the personal touch. Technology can do great things to aid your productivity and efficiency, but it can't offer the personal touch; only you can do that.

BLOGS

Blogs are something I regularly get asked about – should I write a blog? And to be honest that's not a decision I can make for you. I've seen successful freelancers who have blogs and successful ones who don't. It will depend on both you and what services you are offering. A blog is a hungry monster that needs regular feeding with new, interesting stories and points of view. Think hard about whether you can commit to doing this and doing it well. More importantly, think about what you are trying to achieve by writing a blog.

If you're in the digital marketing space then there may be more pressure for you to put your money where your mouth is. But beware; a blog that hasn't been updated in ages is worse than no blog at all.

Of course, it's ultimately about drumming up new business – but a blog is much more subtle than that. It's about you having a voice and a lens through which you look at the world and want to share, free of charge. Just make sure you keep something behind to sell. Think about how loud a voice you have in your sector and what appetite your customer segments might have for what you say.

Assuming you do want to take the plunge with a blog, a good strategy is to map out the first six months of blog posts at the outset. If you plan to post something new every two weeks, you'll need thirteen detailed posts. Can you come up with thirteen topics? Write up at least the first three or four in full before you even start posting. That way you will have something up your sleeve for those super busy weeks that leave you with no time. And, keep up with your writing so you can stay as far ahead as possible.

PRESENTATIONS AND PROPOSALS

Presentations and proposals are another means to articulate your vision in a bespoke way for clients. With all the copy you've written already you will find that you now have large parts of your proposals and presentations in place; you just need to edit and trim judiciously. Less is more!

Prepare proposal and presentation templates leaving gaps for where the client-specific copy can be added in. This way, even at your busiest you should be able to quickly and accurately send out a proposal for new work. Take some time now to lay these out properly.

If you want to go further, you can also write some bespoke copy for specific customer segments. This is particularly useful if you regularly sell the same service to similar clients.

Why not have a full proposal and presentation ready to go? All you need do is insert the client name and your pricing and your proposal is done. It takes some up-front planning, but think how much time you can save in the future.

BUSINESS CARDS

The final and perhaps the most vital promotional item is your business card. There is no excuse *ever* for not having these to hand wherever you go – business or pleasure. You never know who you are going to meet.

These days you can design and purchase them online at very reasonable prices, so buy in bulk. A business card should carry your name, company name (if you have one) and contact details (phone number, email address, website and possibly social media handles). If you want to bring some more personality to it you can add your logo, an image of yourself, your strapline and so on. Use both sides of the card. Make them as plain or as beautiful as you want, just don't leave them gathering dust in a drawer. A business card is both your simplest promotional tool and one of your most effective.

SUMMARY

The marketing mix gives you a *structure* for your marketing activities. When you first start marketing it can feel very unfocussed, a bit of this and a bit of that. No real reason or framework. Copying what others are doing. No way to measure what is working for you and what isn't.

Taking the time to work on an overall marketing plan for your business will reap rewards and give you the confidence and the knowledge to see what is and what isn't working – and therefore you can change and adapt in a structured way. But you do need to stick to the structure, otherwise you risk doing only those bits you enjoy.

Promotion in the marketing mix wraps up the articulating activities for your marketing plan. You now need the final P, place (also known as distribution), which is how you tell the world you are here.

7.

PUTTING YOUR PLANS INTO ACTION

Before going into the detail of how you'll plan and execute your distribution activities you need to get your online presence up and running. The first thing to consider is your email correspondence.

ACQUIRING A PROFESSIONAL EMAIL ADDRESS

Every freelancer needs a professional email address. It doesn't need to be complicated or costly but it must appear businesslike. If you have your own internet domain (see next section), then you can use that, but there's nothing wrong with using everyday mail providers such as Hotmail, iCloud or Gmail either. Whichever route you choose, avoid using nicknames and/or other informalities in addresses and always include your name, for example:

[firstname].[lastname]@
[firstname]_[lastname]@
[firstname][lastname]@
[firstinitial][lastname]@
[firstinitial].[lastname]@ . . .

You get the idea. If you are using one of the free mail providers and all your combinations are already taken, you will need to differentiate either with an added number or perhaps a tag descriptive of your work, e.g. [myname].Photographer@.

A professional email allows you to separate your work and personal emails and keep your business correspondence easily accessible.

There are plenty of free options, but I'd suggest choosing a well-known provider that will be around for the long term. Alternatively, you can register your own domain and set up an email address from there.

REGISTERING A DOMAIN

Your first port of call should be a domain name registrar such as fasthosts or 1&1 Ionos. (You will find many others online.) As well as your specific domain name (e.g. joebloggs) you will need to consider which top-level domain (TLD) you want to follow it. There are many TLDs to choose from: joebloggs.com, joebloggs.co.uk, joebloggs.org, joebloggs.net etc. etc. If you intend to work mainly in one country then a TLD for that country can be a good option. Search for your chosen domain name and TLD combination to find out whether it is available and, if so, how much it will cost you to register it.

The domain you register for your website should reflect the Brand Me name you decided on at the start of the previous chapter. You might need to get creative if your preferred domain name is already taken. Again, the solution to this is to use a suffix that signifies your sector or specialism, for example joebloggsdigital.com or joebloggsdesign.co.uk.

As well as registering a domain name you'll need some hosting for your website, and you may also want to have your email address associated with your domain. Many domain registrars offer these services. Some also offer simple drag-and-drop website builder options too. It's worth doing your research on what is available from whom, how much the various packages cost and how well they are reviewed. Some web-hosting companies are far easier to deal with than others and if you aren't very technical it's wise to choose one that offers good support.

PUBLISHING YOUR WEBSITE

Once you've registered your domain you can get your website live. You've written your copy already, which is the majority of the work. Now it's time for the techie bit where you work out what platform builder you will use for your website.

If there is no website builder option from your domain provider, choose one of the common platforms such as WordPress, Squarespace or Wix. If, like me, you aren't very technically minded, it might be worth hiring someone to do this bit for you. If that isn't an option, at least choose a website builder platform that doesn't require coding (Squarespace and Wix are in this category), although you should bear in mind that the simpler the user interface is, the less customizable it will be.

If you decide to hire a website designer, make sure they understand what you need *now*. You won't need a hugely complex site just yet, but you'll want the facility to add news articles, testimonials and/or blog posts yourself, rather than pay them to do this.

Most site-building platforms offer 'themes' – customizable templates for websites that take a lot of the work (and coding) out of designing your web presence. Some platforms charge extra for these, some include them free, some offer a mixture of both. Look at the structure you planned in the previous chapter and choose one that fits best with the copy and images you plan to post.

The next stage is to get your site up online ('publishing' it; your web hosting company will provide instructions). Don't forget to include your contact details; if people can't contact you there is no point in having a website.

The final stage, which many people make the mistake of leaving out, is tracking who's coming to your site and what they are doing when they get there. One of the simplest ways to do this is to use Google Analytics. If you set this up correctly from the start you can gather useful data about your visitors that you can use to shape your online marketing strategy.

SEO (SEARCH ENGINE OPTIMIZATION)

SEO is becoming increasingly sophisticated, and whilst the techniques that large companies employ to get to the top of the rankings are less relevant for freelancers, there are some basics you should cover, particularly as SEO is now more personalized to the searcher than ever.

There are three simple ways to improve your rankings:

- Make sure your website is 'responsive' so that it displays nicely on desktops, tablets and mobiles (a good theme should take care of this for you).
- Regularly add new content to the home page such as news or blog posts (Google will rank regularly updated sites higher in its rankings).
- Register your services on Google My Business; this allows you to take charge of what people see when they do a local search for businesses like yours.

SETTING UP YOUR SOCIAL MEDIA

Alongside your website, the other major part of your online presence is your social media activity. If you already have a social media presence in your personal life, think about how you use those media and whether you should separate your personal and professional social media identities.

If you answer yes to either of the following two questions, then I would suggest you consider separating your social media identities:

- Do you have lots of public banter with your friends on social media?
- Do you share pictures and information about your personal life online?

Neither is likely to show you in your best professional light, so would be better kept private.

Embarking on a freelance career is an ideal time to separate your identities on social media and build up your professional identity as you grow your career. For those who remember the world before social media this can be harder as your personal and professional connections can be a little more intertwined, but it's not impossible to do. Clients who are also friends will probably be happy to connect with you in both a personal and professional capacity.

WHICH PLATFORMS ARE RIGHT FOR ME?

This is where you need to do some research into where the people in your sector lurk on social media. The main platforms that you want to consider are Facebook, LinkedIn, Twitter and Instagram plus possibly YouTube and Pinterest.

The media types I know mainly hang out on Facebook, where personal and professional are happy to mingle, and few use LinkedIn. Those in more corporate sectors tend to silo their social media activities, using Facebook solely for personal stuff and LinkedIn and Twitter as their go-to professional social media tools.

Put your professional hat on as you do your research; look at all the platforms and see where you can find most people from your sector and most potential clients. More importantly, note where the professional interactions are taking place.

Prioritize your platforms. Keeping on top of social media is a time-consuming activity, so choose carefully which platforms you engage with. If you are looking at LinkedIn and/or Facebook, you'll also want to consider whether you set up a company page alongside your professional profile. Pick just a couple to concentrate on initially.

My two priority social media platforms are:
1:
2:

This doesn't preclude your participating on other platforms. It just prioritizes your time. There are tools you can use to publish a single posting across multiple social media accounts at the same time. Whilst on the surface these look like time savers, remember that each platform has its own culture and tone of voice, so content splashed across all of them simultaneously might not have the same effect as carefully crafted posts that are platform specific.

Now that you have an online presence, it's time to get on with the actual work of distribution.

DISTRIBUTION

Distribution is the channel through which your clients find your services. There are a multitude of distribution channels, and you need to identify those that will best suit your work and will maximize your impact with minimal cost and effort.

Your distribution activity is all about you getting in front of people, both when they are looking for someone like you (*pull strategy*) and when they don't know they need you (*push strategy*).

The distribution channels can be either online (databases, social media, email) or offline (partnerships/alliances, self-promotion, publicity, word of mouth), and you will need to make use of both.

In your 3Cs analysis, when you researched your competition and how people found them, what you were looking at was their distribution strategy. You might need to reinvent the wheel for your work, you might not: when I was running Girls Angels I used to great advantage distribution channels that were very similar to those of my competition, even though our messaging was completely different: they were selling bike licences and I was selling dreams.

Some distribution activities are best suited for maintaining existing clients and some for finding new ones. You won't know which until you try. Just remember that when you *do* receive an inquiry from a new client, you should make sure you learn how they found you or you won't know which of your marketing activities are working.

GETTING THE WORD OUT ONLINE

Distribution in this sense means providing 'signposts' online that will enable your potential customers to find you. Being registered with relevant online databases and having a social media presence are two ways to link people with your website.

Put yourself in a potential client's shoes; where might *they* look to find services such as yours? Would they just Google, or go down a different route? Once they have become a client, will your future business relationship be purely transactional in nature or is *personal service* the key?

The majority of freelancers I've worked with find that their relationships are based on the personal service they deliver. So, your website, although essential to your distribution is not a distribution strategy per se.

Your distribution strategy is about how you push your message out and get it in front of existing and potential clients. Remember, as with the other three Ps, if you offer more than one service then these all need to be treated individually.

Online databases allow you to register your services and contact details with (usually) other related and/or relevant freelancers and companies. They can also be geographically focussed as a one-stop shop for local services. For example: as a producer I make sure I am listed on local databases for film crews as I wish to do this work locally and so primarily market my services locally. Try Googling your service in your town to discover the databases your potential customers might be consulting.

When you do register with an online database and fill in your details remember that, when a potential client reads it, it will be their first interaction with you and your services. Be sure to articulate clearly what you are offering and keep your information up to date. Different databases have different business models. Some charge users to register, some offer a freemium model, where basic services are free and you can pay for more advanced options (LinkedIn is a good example of this).

Some sites will prioritize its members by availability or by amount of activity on the site, so if you do rely on that type of site then make sure you play the game and do a quick login at the start of each day to keep your position in their rankings.

You will have to work out which services are worth paying for and which aren't. You need to think about how you are going to measure return on investments like this, so you know which ones are the most effective for you. It's very unlikely that one database alone will be the source of all your work. Also, if I'm a client looking for your services and searching through a series of online databases for a potential supplier, I am going to notice if your name comes up repeatedly across a series of searches.

SOCIAL MEDIA

Whilst a professional social media presence is important, just like your website that is not a distribution strategy in itself. Within social media you distribute by pushing your voice out there and making people take notice of you. It's about getting the right message in front of the right person at the right time.

The first step is to post on your own timeline. Make your posts useful, relevant and professional. It doesn't all need to be written and crafted by you (although the more original content you can come up with, the better), but can also include sharing useful information, articles and events with your professional networks. Sharing demonstrates that you have your finger on the pulse of your sector and are the go-to person for information on what's happening.

Write down all the useful sources of information and articles for your sector of work. They could be newspapers, trade press, sector bodies, public sector organizations, bloggers, other freelancers or influencers. These will form the core of the knowledge you want to gather. It will be useful for your market insight when dealing with clients and can also provide you with shareable content for your audience.

Posting regularly on your social media platforms is all well and good, but you are only reaching a limited number of people who are already in your networks. If you want to use social media to engage with a wider audience and as a means of drumming up new clients, then you need to engage with forums and groups.

FORUMS AND GROUPS

Forums and groups are spaces on social media where like-minded people chat and share knowledge and opportunities. They are places where you can engage in conversation with a much wider audience.

You may find that being part of the industry conversation and being your helpful self is time better spent than posting on your timeline. Just look at the numbers of people following you personally versus the number in an industry group. There are likely to be more in the industry group and you're also reaching outside your existing network, so balance your time between your own posting and joining in the conversation on active forums and groups.

#HASHTAGS

Hashtags are another important way to connect your views and conversations with a wider audience. Most social media platforms allow you to search via hashtags. They are a great way to search for information and see what people are saying on a subject.

Do your research on what your sector, including your competition, are using as hashtags. Come up with your own shortlist that you will use regularly to promote your offer. You might want a balance between bespoke and generic hashtags so both can be found in a wider conversation but also stand out.

It's important to keep your online presence up to date and be seen to be active. That said, be wary of the super prolific Twitterer or Facebooker who never stops posting – it makes them look like they've got no work!

EMAIL

A final online distribution channel to examine is email. And yes, it is a distribution channel – what you write in your email is a promotional activity but the act of hitting 'send' is distribution. It's easy to underestimate the distribution opportunity that email offers. Relationship management software can track the effectiveness of your emails including open and click-through rates by contact. In addition to tracking contact activity there is also technology to handle your marketing correspondence from simple online email newsletters to full marketing automation. It's worth doing your research to see which software is most suitable for your needs.

Capsule CRM, for example, is predominantly a contact management software, and for more sophisticated marketing automation services there are MailChimp and Mautic, to name but two. Of course, none of these is a magic pill. You get out what you put in. By taking the time to organize your contacts database inside the software at the start you will reap the most rewards.

One facilitator I know recently decided to use one of these packages and before she even sent a tracked email, she had completely changed her thinking on a whole host of people in her address book. Taking the time to assign different contacts to different categories (such as new leads or past clients) gave her a new outlook on her networks. She could start to think about promoting herself to them and positioning her offering according to which category she'd put them in.

Visibility across a range of online channels is important, but will not secure sales directly in an offline market. That's up to you and how you pitch yourself once you're in front of clients. It doesn't matter how good your online presence is, you still sell yourself to real people. Business was being done that way for centuries before the internet and social media came along. It worked then and it works now.

OFFLINE

Leaving cyberspace for the real world, your potential distribution channels revolve around people – who you know, your relationships with them and where you meet them.

Companies can be very cautious about finding new people to work with. Many freelancing engagements fall outside formal procurement and hiring protocols. When looking for a freelancer, people prefer to use someone they know and can trust. They'll step outside this comfort zone only as a distress purchase when all their regulars are busy, or if they are venturing into a new area of work.

Even then, finding a new freelancer is often still done through recommendation, so when a client asks someone if they know anyone who does your particular type of work, you want yours to be the name they're given.

SELF-PROMOTION

You are the one who cares most about you getting work, and you are the best person to sell your services. Own it and sell it. You need to get out there and tell the world what you are up to as you can't rely on others to do it for you.

It sounds trite, but always sounding positive will get you a long way. It's those lasting impressions you make on people. It gets around if you're moody or 'difficult'. Yes, such behaviour might be tolerated for a while, but someone will always come along who can do similar work with a smile.

It always used to be said that you should appear busy, but life is so full these days that being busy is a given. Instead, I focus on sounding positive and interesting. Think about the person you are talking to and have a nugget of something that will whet their appetite and make them want to hear more about what you are doing and why. Once you've got them hooked, make sure you hand them a business card and get one in return so you can follow up.

Self-promotion is all about communicating *Why me?* in both an online and an offline environment. Listening is a very powerful tool. If you listen to a client and can hear what their problem is, you may be able to come up with a novel solution to it.

WORD OF MOUTH

If you can build a strong reputation among clients and other colleagues then you may well be able to create your own personal word-of-mouth distribution channel.

Freelancing is a people-to-people activity, so the stronger your word-of-mouth channel is, the better. These are your sponsors, the people talking about you when you are not in the room.

PARTNERSHIPS AND ALLIANCES

Partnerships and alliances build on your word of mouth. They can be formal or informal arrangements whereby you cross-promote each other's services. For example, a graphic designer might have a preferred printing company that they use and will be likely to recommend them to clients. In return the printing company will make cross-recommendations to any of their customers seeking a graphic designer.

When I ran Girls Angels, I worked very hard on our informal alliances. I placed leaflets in local motorbike and scooter shops, which they distributed to suitable customers. In return, our instructors included those shops on their training routes so that our clients could inspect the bikes and scooters they had for sale. This was a case of mutual need and mutual benefit. Think about where and how you can cross-promote with other freelancers.

ADVERTISING

Whilst traditional spot advertising on TV is unlikely to be realistic, there are lower cost and more targeted opportunities that you might want to consider when promoting your freelancer services, such as local magazines or websites and/or trade-specific publications.

If you feel strongly that you have many potential customers in your local area that you want to reach, do your research and identify opportunities to advertise your message to them. If there is a specific sector you are looking to develop then, again, it can pay (pardon the pun) to place an advertisement in relevant trade publications. That said, a well-written press release can get you as much space in a publication as an advert, and with substantially greater impact.

The key to any publicity campaign is to know who you are trying to reach with your advert and then to measure as best you can its ROI (return on investment) – in other words, how much have you gained in return for the cost of the advert?

The usual way to monitor ROI is to ask anyone who inquires about your services where they heard about you. We made a point of doing this rigorously with Girls Angels and we quickly built up a picture of which of our advertising and marketing efforts were working best. If you do plan to invest some money into advertising, use the ALTR analysis you did earlier to ensure that the advertising message you are sending out corresponds to the step you want your potential customers to take.

Social media can be a great platform on which to advertise your services and will push you hard to boost posts that you have made. Whilst this type of advertising can be very successful, it takes time and thought to craft a well-written post for your intended audience and then some more time to drill down into the specifics of who you are targeting. A simple boost on a post will merely optimize for more engagement with your post rather than clicks through to your site.

PUBLICITY

Publicity is any unpaid form of mass-media communication about a product or a service, such as a news story about you or what you do. Whilst you could engage the services of a PR company, this can be expensive and for a small operation is akin to using a sledgehammer to crack a nut. Skilfully placed and creatively used publicity can generate tremendous impact for you at very low cost.

Think about the customer segments you are already working in and consider the trade press that services them. Most companies will want to have good-news stories about them featured in their trade press. It keeps their brand at the forefront and makes them look good. If you can put together a joint news story about the work you've done, how it is innovative and has transformed an aspect of their business, then it's a win–win. The client is happy because they are getting a good story about themselves in their trade press. You are building brand awareness in a sector showing how good your work is and getting your name in front of all your client's competitors.

Unlike traditional advertising, these stories cost nothing to place and they can be extremely effective. They are given more credence by readers because they are editorial.

SUMMARY

Distribution is the act of getting the right message out there across the right channels for the right customer segment. Remember that your different customer segments may well require different approaches when it comes to distribution as well as different messages.

Placing your product or service is the final ingredient in the 4Ps marketing mix. It brings together your research and provides the channels through which you articulate your vision.

It's where you put your plans into action.

Remember that marketing and sales are different but closely linked. In simple terms, marketing is everything you do to *reach* a potential client and get *noticed* by them, then the sales process is what kicks in once you're in front of that *potential* client to turn them into a *paying* client.

Marketing informs sales about *who* the customers are, *where* to find them and *what* price they are prepared to pay. The most important thing is to **plan** it and then **follow the plan**. Without a structured marketing plan your marketing and subsequent sales activities can feel random and you will find the process both difficult and ineffective.

Now that you've completed your marketing planning, the time has come to actively sell your services. The first step in the process is prospecting for customers, and the next chapter looks at how you can use your network to do so.

8.

NURTURING AND LEVERAGING YOUR NETWORK

Now it's time to get some *actual paying customers*. Many people find this daunting, but you've done the difficult bits, so now it's time for all that hard work to fall into place.

First, you need to do some prospecting. This means compiling lists of potential customers and their contact details. It's also about looking for places and events where these prospects come together so you can get in front of them – and sell to them.

WHAT IS YOUR 'NETWORK'?

Your network is your single most important asset when looking for work and you should never underestimate its value. The anthropologist Robin Dunbar suggests that there is a limit to the number of people with whom anyone can maintain a close relationship. It's now known as Dunbar's number, and it proposes that humans can comfortably maintain only about 150 stable relationships. He defines these as people you would not feel embarrassed about joining uninvited for a drink if you happened to bump into them in a bar.

So, let's assume you have 150 people in your network and each person in your network has 150 relationships. This means that there are 22,500 (150 × 150) people at one degree of separation from you. That's a lot of people who could potentially be your customers. And the more established you are, the more likely your network will have customers (or potential customers) in it.

As you can see, even if you are starting out and feel like you have a small personal network, the reality is that it is bigger than you think. The trick is to know how to extract the maximum value from it.

IDENTIFYING YOUR PERSONAL NETWORK

Your personal network comprises your friends and family, colleagues from courses you've been on, people you've worked alongside as a co-worker, client or supplier – in fact, more or less anyone you've had a good working or personal relationship with, past or present.

The easiest way to start is to set up a spreadsheet categorizing the information so that it's easy to sort. This is simple to manipulate and easily exported to other software later on. You can also subcategorize to sort more easily; for example the category 'friend' could have subcategories 'school', 'university', 'family' etc. Add an additional column for that extra detail. Taking time to put your network in order now will reap the rewards later on.

Your LinkedIn profile has one list of connections, your Facebook account will have another list. Your mobile phone has a contacts list. Your email software has an address book. You'll have 'met' people on other social media platforms or forums. Some of these will be friends, some work colleagues, others completely new, but to qualify for inclusion in your list they should be people you've had meaningful interactions with and/or with whom you are actively discussing ideas and opportunities relevant to your work.

Once you've pulled all these lists together, consider who might be able to act as an introducer as well as who might be able to offer you work directly, and create categories for them too. Keep data protection legislation in mind and make sure you are handling this data securely. Password-protecting the file is prudent.

At this stage you are just looking to identify all the people who are already in your network and who know you.

To summarize, your spreadsheet should contain the following columns:

- Name
- Contact details
- Type of relationship (with subcategories)
- Whether they are a potential client or introducer. (If an introducer, subcategorize according to the sort of people they are likely to be able to introduce you to. If a potential customer, subcategorize according to their customer segment.)

In addition to the above:

- Give each contact a priority number based on how influential an introducer might be or the importance you place on the work a potential customer might offer.
- For a portfolio career – add an additional column to your spreadsheet to outline which part of your portfolio offering this contact relates to.
- Add a column for primary contact method – phone, email, social media, face-to-face or something else.

Now you have your list properly categorized you can use the sort function to sort it in any way you choose. Sorting by priority is the foundation for your 'to do' list when prospecting for customers.

This list is the start of your customer database. It is a place to keep all your contact information and the latest stage of your discussions.

Keeping notes on your interaction with each prospect is important – reach out, allow time to respond, reach out again, allow time etc. If on the third approach you don't hear back you might want to consider whether your approach is working.

There are many useful software and online applications that can help you with your *customer relationship management* (CRM). Traditionally these have been designed for companies employing teams that need to share information, so they can be overcomplex for one person's needs, but there are now products available that are better set up for freelancers, such as InfoFlo.

As well as holding all your contacts in a categorized fashion they can be set up to perform as a 'virtual assistant' and remind you who you need to reach out to and when. They aren't psychic – you'll need to input this information first – but once you've done that you'll get regular prompts. If you think you are someone who isn't well organized or will shy away from reaching out to people, buying such a package could be time and money well spent.

SPONSORS, MENTORS AND COACHES

As well as being a source of business or leads your network is likely to be filled with people who can support you in other ways. Consider those who could act as either sponsors, mentors or coaches for you.

A **sponsor** is someone who talks about you when you're not in the room. These people are my favourite: they are your own personal distribution channel, referring and recommending you whilst you are doing something else – hopefully earning money on another project or sleeping. Networks and recommendations are vital for freelancers, so think about who you act as a sponsor for, and who can act as a sponsor for you. Think about how you can build on this.

Remember, it's not just about who's being *your* sponsor. If you get a name for being someone who knows lots of good people and makes good recommendations, the phone will ring as people seek your advice. Being that great sponsor for others is also a successful marketing activity for yourself. Word of mouth is an extremely important distribution channel and is very valuable.

Mentors are those who have more experience than you in your field and are great people to have supporting you, particularly when starting out. They can also be a source of referrals. Think about it: they are experienced professionals; they are probably pretty busy and they may well be in demand with all sorts of clients.

Mentors can offer a level of insight it is hard to achieve when you work on your own, so finding a person or – even better – a few people who will give you time periodically can be extremely valuable. There might be opportunities for you to collaborate with them. They may even introduce you to clients they can't support because of time pressures or because the client has too limited a budget.

Think about the people in your network you would consider as mentors. What is your relationship like with them? Perhaps someone who was a guest lecturer on your course really inspired you. Get in touch with them and see if they will mentor you. They will usually be looking to help those starting out and/or will be keen to meet new talent – that's often why they agree to lecture to students. People are much more receptive to mentoring than you might think.

Mentors can support you with further developing your expertise in your field. You don't have to be starting out to have a mentor. They are hugely valuable at all stages of your career.

Coaches, on the other hand, are those people in your networks who can support you on a *personal* level. The people you can talk through personal challenges with and who will help you see the wood for the trees. These people are often outside your direct area of work for obvious reasons and needn't be professional 'life coaches'; more often these will be friendship-based conversations.

GROWING YOUR NETWORK

When you've pulled together a detailed list of everyone in your network, ask yourself which of your target customer segments you have established networks in, and which need nurturing and developing. Focus your network-building efforts on these weaker network areas, particularly if this is one of the priority customer segments you identified earlier.

Having identified your current network and where the gaps might be, you next go about filling them by – what else? – networking.

NETWORKING EVENTS

Networking events are a key part of building your professional networks.

Networking isn't everyone's favourite pastime. It is hard work, but the good networkers I speak to say it's all in the preparation. Know what event you are going to and why you are going. As with any decision you make concerning your business, you could and should subject it to a cost–benefit analysis. What is the cost to my business if I go to this event? What benefit might I get out of it? If the likely potential benefits outweigh the cost then there is a good reason to go.

Prepare by doing your homework thoroughly. Know who's presenting and what they will be talking about. See who else is going. Once you have a handle on the content, think about some of the talking points you might raise as well as questions. They are great ice-breakers when you first get to the event.

There are generally two reasons to go to an event or a conference:

1. To gain information – is the event or conference covering a topic you want to know more about?
2. To meet people – do you want to network with the people who will be attending the event or conference as they are influential and/or of potential benefit to your business?

If an event's primary goal is to offer information it will attract people like you looking for the same information. Thus you will meet people who work in similar areas to you and could develop relationships with potential collaborators.

An event you go to at which you expect to meet useful people is one where you'll want to be raising your profile about what you do and why you do it.

A really good event will satisfy both aims.

You can usually divide events into two parts – *information dissemination* and the *bits in between*. Both give you opportunities to make your voice heard.

During the information dissemination stage you can create awareness of yourself by volunteering to sit on a panel. Failing that, ask an informed and intelligent question when the opportunity arises. That's where doing your homework comes in.

If you do ask a question at an event, it's good practice to start by giving your name and what you do as it helps the panel and the audience understand your perspective (and, of course, it promotes you). And please make sure it is a question. At all costs, don't grab the mic and just make a long-winded statement. If your opinion was required, you'd be on the panel.

Don't ignore the *bits in between* – they are vital to your network building. This is where you need to work the room hard and meet as many people as you can. My mentor, Mike Southon, is the best networker I've ever met and has very straightforward advice about how to do this type of networking. He asks five questions in a logical order, and this stood me in very good stead in my first start-up at a time when I knew hardly anyone in the sector.

The key according to Mike is to get into the conversation, ascertain quickly who might be worth following up with and then get out of the conversation and move on to the next group. That way you can talk to as many people as possible, maximizing the number of good leads you secure.

To get started, all you need do is go up to a group of people chatting and simply ask, 'May I join you?'

Nearly always the reply will be, 'Of course.' (If not, just move on. Chances are you wouldn't want to be working with them anyway.) Then come the five questions:

QUESTION 1:

'*Where* are you based?' – a simple opener to get the conversation going.

QUESTION 2:

'*What* do you do?' – a simple question inviting a simple, factual answer. When they ask you the 'what' question back you should be ready with your client-focussed pitch.

QUESTION 3:

'*How* does that work, exactly?' – this is a more probing question about them or their company. If it's already feeling like hard work, this is your cue to move on. Ask for a business card and politely say, 'It was nice chatting to you; if you don't mind, I'm going to get another drink . . .' However, if the conversation is going well you can move on to the next question.

QUESTION 4:

'*Why* are you here?' – this is an emotional rather than factual inquiry and you are hoping they will open up to you. This will give you the chance to offer them a 'fact' – it could be a book, a website, an article you think would help them. It's where you show them your value. If they refuse it, then it's time to move politely on.

QUESTION 5:

'*Who* can I introduce you to?' – by this time you've gathered that you are on the same page with this person and that you like each other. So, even if you can't directly help them, by offering to introduce them to someone you know who could, you are showing your value – this time to both your new acquaintance and the person in your network.

All you need do after the event is ensure you follow up on all the good contacts made. A useful trick is, as soon as the discussion finishes, to write on each person's business card what you discussed so you have the information to hand when you send them a follow-up email.

Following up should always be done **the next day**. Get into the habit of keeping business cards in one place when you are given them and as soon as you are back at your desk put them where you can see them for immediate follow-up before filing them away.

And then, once you've sent that email, you may need to follow up again. This is where your contact management system comes into its own; update it with these new contacts and it does the heavy lifting for you and tells you what to do when.

DIFFERENTIATING AMONG TYPES OF EVENTS

As well as knowing how to network when you get to an event you need to be clear on the differences between different types of events – seminars, workshops, conferences and trade shows. They will vary by cost of entry and size of event – with seminars and workshops being the smallest and generally lowest cost, and trade shows the largest and most expensive.

SEMINARS

Seminars are generally held to build attendees' knowledge. They can be ad hoc events and are usually small, with a token or no admission charge. This means there may be fewer people to meet overall but you are likely to have more time to talk to all of them. Seminars are usually informational sessions where people go to learn and develop knowledge in an informal environment.

Look for local seminars to start with. Not all will work for you, but at least you won't have spent too much time or money getting there or getting in.

WORKSHOPS

Like seminars, workshops tend to be quite small. Prices can range from no cost to pricey. They are usually run in small groups for half a day or longer, even over several days. Workshops are inherently interactive learning environments. They are facilitated by an expert and the attendees are there to learn. All will have identified similar issues that the workshop is there to help with. The network of people you meet on workshops can be as valuable to you as the information that the facilitator delivers. Workshops offer good opportunities to engage in dialogue and ask questions. Again, start by looking locally.

CONFERENCES

Conferences are larger, more formal occasions attracting a broad cross-section of an industry and leading figures to speak, so they are a place where people come together, often from across the country, or even internationally.

Conferences are good places both to receive information and to meet people. There are always breaks between sessions during which you can mingle and talk, and usually some drinks at the end of the day as well. When you plan your conference trip make sure you give yourself time to take full advantage of these opportunities. The end of the day can be the most valuable time if you are prospecting for customers. People are relaxed, they've got a drink and they are happy to chat, so make the most of it.

If you can't afford the admission fee, a great way to get involved is as a volunteer. It's also an effective short cut to meeting established players in the sector. Many conferences and events use volunteers in a whole range of roles – producing sessions, live blogging or tweeting, organizing, staffing the registration desk etc.

They won't pay you (obviously!), but they'll often give you a conference pass in lieu – which is generally the reason you are volunteering in the first place. If you find yourself on the registration desk you will meet everyone who attends, and if you've done your homework and have a target list of people to talk to, you can use the opportunity to ask for a few minutes of their time later on. (The 'later on' part is important: you've volunteered to do a job; it looks highly unprofessional to be networking and registering people at the same time!)

For the more experienced, being on a panel at a conference can bring you to the attention of many potential clients at once and allows you to position yourself as an expert.

PUBLIC SPEAKING

As you build up your reputation and expertise there comes a point when being on a panel stops being a sales exercise for you and people start coming to the conference at least partly because you are speaking. If public speaking is an income stream that you want to develop, you don't want to be doing it for nothing. Are you selling your services or are you the draw that's helping to sell tickets? If it's the latter, then make clear to the organizers what your terms are for speaking. Conference organizers can be very reticent about offering fees to speakers and opaque about who or what they pay. It's up to you to do your research and take stock of each individual conference and who the intended audience is before you agree your terms for taking part.

This is where agents come in. If you are forging a speaking career then an agent might be just what you need to support you. Yes, they take a percentage of your earnings, but the higher fees they negotiate for you should more than cover that and they ought to obtain more work for you than you could attract by yourself. (That aside, it can also be a relief not to be the person discussing money, allowing you to concentrate on the work in hand.)

There are many different types of agent, so do your research and pick one that's right for you.

TRADE SHOWS

Trade shows are the most formal type of networking event. A marketplace where people are looking to meet and do deals. Companies take stands to showcase their products and services. Buyers circulate, looking to see what is new and what interests them. Exhibiting is expensive and there is no guarantee that it's the right place for you, so it's better to start by attending as a delegate and seeing how the show works; then at least you are in a position to make an informed decision for the following year. Many set aside an area for newcomers to the field, so look out for those as well – they are often discounted accordingly.

Trade shows are big business and the organizers employ experienced sales people to sell stands at their conferences. Their motive is simply to see the space filled, so don't let their persuasive arguments push you into taking a stand at a trade show, particularly one you've never been to.

Increasingly, trade show programmes include breakout seminars to provide attendees with further sector knowledge, so they can be very useful to attend if only for these. You can talk to the exhibitors, but if you aren't really looking to buy you may find them unwilling to enter into conversation with you. After all, they've paid a lot of money to exhibit and they are there to sell. If you're not a potential customer, they aren't going to be interested.

Whatever type of event you are thinking of going to, before you book anything make sure you are clear *why you are going* and *what you hope to gain* by attending. Is it for information or to meet people? Your skills audit results are a great starting point to help you identify seminars and workshops that will deliver the skills and knowledge you are hoping to gain.

IDENTIFYING OPPORTUNITIES TO DEVELOP YOUR NETWORKS

Effective network development requires an understanding of the sort of people you want to meet. From there, you can plan the best type of events to go to.

Do your online research – find organizations that bring together information on a sector, sign up to their newsletters, follow them on social media. Most of these organizations are keen to let their subscribers know about events and news that have relevance to them.

Importantly, read what is sent to you. If you aren't finding it useful then you can always unsubscribe.

There are also event platforms such as Eventbrite and Meetup that promote and manage ticket sales for events. Many of these are open events that you can search for by area and by topic.

Target those customer segments you are trying to build your networks in. To do this, consider what sort of events and conferences would attract people in those segments. Concentrate for now on informational events. These are easier to identify and are likely to get the largest number of target customers, so will give you the most people to talk to. Start locally and build out from there.

As well as looking to see what is out there for your sector, investigate whether there is an established community of freelancers near you. If there is, it's likely there is some sort of regular group meeting. If not, you can be the person to get something going. It doesn't have to be formal. It could start as a group of like-minded people getting together in a pub or café once a month and discussing the challenges of working for yourself.

LOOK AFTER YOURSELF!

If you are at a big and/or long event over a few days it's important you look after yourself. Learn your limitations. There's no point being in the room if you're overtired and all talked out. You won't do yourself justice. Take the day in short bursts. It's completely usual to need a little time out from the crowd to recharge – take five minutes to get some fresh air, have a walk round the block and escape the mayhem. Then, come back in refreshed, with a smile on your face and ready to go again.

Be nice, be interested and be interesting. Have your talking points ready. Just like in comedy, timing is everything, so read the situation for an opportunity to pitch yourself and be open to others' pitches to you.

Whatever you do, don't stand there looking at your phone,

waiting for people to talk to you. They won't. You'll come across as aloof and disinterested and closed to opportunity.

DATA PROTECTION

When it comes to harvesting and storing data, there are now in nearly every jurisdiction strict laws with which you must comply.

The EU General Data Protection Regulation (GDPR) is thought to be the model framework as far as data protection regulation goes, and although at the time of writing it is not in force globally it has extra-territorial force and is widely expected to become the norm. GDPR applies if you do any work in the European Union, or hold or process data on any individuals based there.

Think of GDPR as a health-and-safety policy for your data handling and management.

GDPR is among the more stringent regulatory frameworks, so if you comply with it then your data management practices should be adequate for most jurisdictions. It is designed to give people more control of their personal and sensitive data and harmonize the rules across the EU. The rules apply to anyone who controls or processes data, meaning that they are likely to affect most businesses, however small – and this includes freelancers. There are two kinds of data: *personal data*, which is anything that could identify an individual (name, IP address, physical address or email address) and *sensitive personal data*, which includes anything from health records to religion, political views or sexual orientation.

GDPR means people can demand that organizations reveal what data is being held about them and also they have a 'right to be forgotten'.

GDPR is likely to affect you in two ways.

The first and most obvious is that you must inform people about any data you collect and keep, what you plan to do with it, and who else might see it. Second, no data may be kept unless the person involved has positively 'opted-in', for example by ticking a box on a contact form on your website. (This is a major change from earlier practice, where companies often ticked agreement boxes by default and people had to opt out by unticking them.)

The two main areas this may affect are:

- Email marketing – fortunately, most automated marketing services are set up to be GDPR compliant, although you should check this if you are using one.
- Subcontracting – this is slightly more onerous; if you are subcontracting or involving others you need to handle their personal data with care.

There is a common misperception that GDPR only affects business-to-consumer transactions. It doesn't. Personal data is personal data, so if you can identify an individual directly or indirectly, then GDPR applies – even if you are acting in a purely professional capacity. So, if you have a name and number of a contact on file, or their email address identifies them, then GDPR applies.

You don't always need *formal* consent to retain information, though. Consent is one lawful basis for processing, but you can also rely on 'legitimate interests' to justify some of your business-to-business marketing or communications, for example emailing an invoice. If you can show your use of people's data is proportionate, has a minimal privacy impact and people would not be surprised or likely to object to what you are doing, you're fine. Note that this does NOT mean that you can undertake unsolicited marketing by phone, fax, email or text if aimed at an individual rather than – for example – an 'info@' email address. In the UK the Information Commissioner's Office has some excellent guidance on these matters.

The second data protection consideration might not seem so obvious but, if anything, it's more important, and it's this: how secure is *your* data? If you are trading under your own name, using your home address for all your business correspondence and possibly using your personal bank account, you might want to reflect on how much personal data you are putting out into the public domain when you are working. Your home address, phone number and email address plus your bank details are on all your invoices.

In this increasingly electronic world it is a good idea to keep a degree of separation between your professional and personal details so you don't broadcast personal information when you don't need to.

SUMMARY

You now have a comprehensive database of your network, a priority list of target customers to contact, an idea of which part of your networks and knowledge you are looking to develop and where you will go to do this.

It's now time to turn your contacts into customers.

9.

TURNING YOUR CONTACTS INTO CUSTOMERS

This is the big step. It's the moment of transition from passive 'marketing' to the active role of selling. It's the first time you will be approaching customers directly.

Many people hate the concept of 'selling' as it seems sort of tacky, but ultimately *if you can't sell yourself you won't succeed*. It's tempting to find something more attractive to do than chasing sales, like rearranging your filing or making sure your admin is up to date. But if you don't have customers you won't have any admin to keep up with. There's no escaping the need to sell. On the plus side, you're selling yourself – so what's not to like?

Being 'sold to' happens all the time. You know what it sounds like – especially when it's heavy-handed and obvious. Coming across as 'hard-selling' to any potential client is deeply unattractive – it's a bit like sounding desperate when you're trying to get a date.

You can break down the marketing-to-sales process into **five essential steps**. Like the dating analogy above, there is a bit of a courtship ritual to it:

1. What does a good customer look like?
2. How do I find them?

3. How do I get them to notice me?
4. How do I get in front of them and make them want to work with me?
5. Once I'm in, *how do I stay there*?

Don't underestimate the importance of that last point; it's much easier selling *more* to an *existing customer* than finding a new one. Any salesperson will tell you that.

The good news is that you've already done the first three in Chapters 3 and 7, so now it is time to look at 4 and 5 – how you get in front of people and what you do when you get there.

SALES FUNNEL

To use sales-and-marketing jargon, this is your sales funnel. The process by which you make potential customers aware of you, pitch to them and ultimately close a deal. Just like a funnel, you need to put a lot in at the top and only a few will filter down at a time. You also need to know where in the funnel each potential customer is: it's usually a good idea to pay more attention to those you are nearer to closing a deal with than those in the early stages. That said, keeping your sales funnel full is crucial to generating new and more sales, so it's a delicate balancing act.

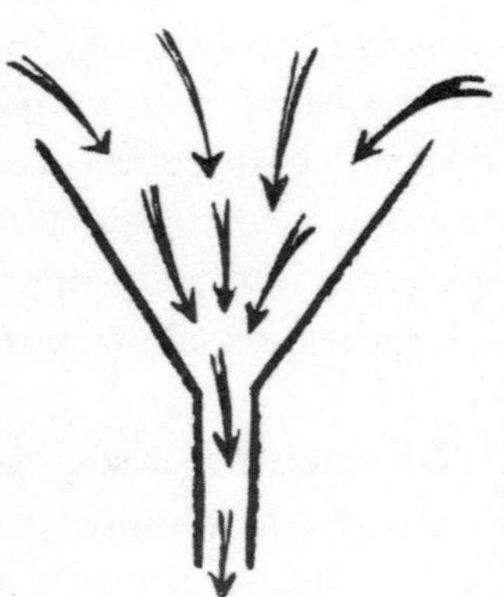

A good example is the traditional job-search process. You send out application form after application form and then suddenly you get a bite. A company has granted you an interview. It's a great job, one you really want, so you stop applying for any others. That's all well and good if you get the job, but if you don't, you've got no applications coming down the funnel, no interviews to come, and you've got to start again from scratch.

It's the same with selling; if you want to keep regular work coming in you need to keep filling the funnel. Otherwise, like the job hunter, your progress will fall off a cliff once your current project is completed.

GETTING IN FRONT OF CUSTOMERS

The first step is to sort your prospect list so that the priority 1 targets are all at the top. Familiarizing yourself now with how to sort, filter and manage your list will pay dividends; whilst it might not be that extensive yet, as it grows it will quickly become unwieldy, making it hard to see at a glance who you should be targeting.

The easiest people to get in front of are those you already know – clients, colleagues, friends or introducer contacts. These people should readily respond to your approaches. Contact them using the primary contact method you determined earlier for each one.

One caveat: when you reach out to your introducer contacts, you aren't selling your services directly to them, you want them to introduce you to people in their networks they think could use your services.

WRITING WINNING EMAILS

Email is a very powerful tool for connecting with your clients and promoting your services. There are two main ways in which you can use it – one-to-many or one-to-one.

One-to-many email marketing newsletters are sent with the intention of getting recipients to click through to a company's website, where they hopefully will buy something. How frequently do you even open one of these, let alone click through? Probably not often. It's a numbers game: you need to have a lot of people who have signed up to your mailing list and you need to send them out regularly. If you have chosen to write a blog then a well-written marketing email can bring it to the attention of those on your distribution list. It can also allow you to position yourself as an expert. As with all things marketing, the trick is to tell a story that engages your customers and is written in a way that makes them see value in it. GDPR means that you can't 'spam' people: they need to have opted-in to receive your pearls of wisdom and also be easily able to opt-out. A good email marketing program or provider will take care of this for you.

When it comes to meeting customers face to face, the one-to-one personal email is the best approach. My mentor Mike Southon has some great advice concerning this: '**It's fifteen seconds to win fifteen minutes**.' What he means is that the email should take no longer than fifteen seconds to read and you should ask for only fifteen minutes of their time. Think of this email as your chat-up line that you hope will lead to a date.

The winning format is pretty straightforward when you break it down. You open the email with a polite hello and follow it with four short lines:

1. **Hook line** – outline the problem you perceive the client to have.
2. **Premise** – I am the best at solving this because . . .
3. **Proof** – talk to this third party, they'll corroborate what I'm saying.
4. **Offer** – how about I come and see you for fifteen minutes on [date and time]?

A brief, well-written email like this will open doors. Don't forget to make your message client-focussed throughout: you're proposing solutions to the customer's problem, not peddling your products from a suitcase.

Just like other forms of sales, writing winning emails is a numbers game. The more you send, the more positive responses you could receive. If you can achieve a 15 per cent success rate then from every hundred emails you should get fifteen meetings. Clearly, the larger your network, the larger your potential rewards.

COLD CALLING

Cold calling is also a numbers game. The more calls you make the more chance you have of getting a meeting. The chances of you calling at just the right moment, when the potential client is thinking they need your services, are witheringly low. Most recipients of a cold call are simply irritated by it. So you have to question if it is an appropriate strategy for getting in front of clients you'd like to build an ongoing relationship with. Additionally, in the UK there are regulations concerning unsolicited calls – companies and individuals can register not to receive them so you'd need to use an online checker prior to picking up the phone. As a strategy, it's probably not time best spent.

APPROACHING PEOPLE ONLINE IN GROUPS AND FORUMS

In some ways, pitching via online groups and forums is a modern version of cold calling. It's now easier than ever to broadcast your message to a customer base you are targeting. There are huge numbers of groups and forums where people with common interests can be found. Active groups can make a lot of noise and often generate lively discussion and comment. The challenge is to find your way into the conversation and get yourself noticed (for the right reasons, of course!).

Every group has its own rules and etiquette, commonly known as a code of conduct, or CoC, and you should make sure you are clear what each one is and that you follow it (CoCs differ from group to group). Before you join the conversation, start by simply familiarizing yourself with the group and taking its temperature (a process known as 'lurking'). Do common themes for discussion arise? Are there a wide number of voices or just a few? Are people genuinely asking advice or are they all selling with little engagement? You can then decide whether the conversation is one that is worth joining and, if so, the best way to go about making a contribution to it.

The groups I join are either general-interest local groups, groups with people like me or groups with people in my target customer segments.

I like to lurk in the groups where conversations are ongoing and people are looking for other members to help them with an issue. These tend to be the groups in which participants are the most engaged and open to new ideas from the community.

When you are ready to join a conversation, read all the previous comments on the thread carefully so that you aren't just rehashing someone else's idea. Be helpful when you comment and be positive. Try to make your posts interesting. If you think the person is asking the wrong question, avoid making a blunt statement to this effect and instead post a tactful response, such as 'Have you thought about it [this way]?' This portrays you as someone who knows what they are talking about and as an enabling, helpful type.

If someone in the group or forum interests you especially, go to their profile page to learn more about them. They could be a potential customer for your services. Use this knowledge to tailor your comments on their posts subtly, to make them notice you (but beware of turning into their stalker . . . it can be a fine line between the two in the online world).

RECORDING YOUR SALES ACTIVITY

When you are selling your services, keep a log of your activities, who you talk to and whether you get the work or not. You can learn a lot from your failures if you take time to reflect on and analyse what you did and why you might have missed out.

There is no harm in asking the client for feedback – especially if you think you were very close to getting the work. You might just get that nugget of information that will turn a no into a yes elsewhere. And remember, when you ask for feedback you really need to listen. This is not an opportunity for you to try to make them change their mind (they've already made the decision, and trying to flog a dead horse will only confirm that they were right). Listen hard to what they have to say. There's a chance you won't like what you hear, but that is exactly the point of the exercise. Honest feedback can transform businesses. It can help you understand not only how you are coming across but also where the pain is for the client. Take it on board.

So, you've made your approaches and secured a face-to-face meeting. Now it's time to get ready to make your first pitch.

Whatever contract, project or role you pitch or interview for, it's worth remembering that you will be working with people, and the people booking your services want to work with someone they think they can get on with. It goes without saying that you must be competent to do the job, but so will all your rivals for the work. The client's eventual decision will be based on fit and whether you have portrayed yourself as a person they want to work with.

PRE-MEETING PREP

Before any meeting there is prep to do. You need to research the company you are going to as well as the people you are meeting. This involves more than a quick glance at their website. Look also at their activity on social media, learn who their clients are, search for news articles, read their financial accounts. There's a lot of information in the public domain once you start digging. It all builds up a picture of the company and will help you to understand their perspective and inform your *Why Me?* when you are in the meeting.

As you do your research, be alert for alarm bells. Could dealing with this company be a potential waste of your time? Does what you have learned make you believe they share your values? If yes, you have some common ground to discuss. If no, then be ready to probe this at the meeting. If you're not going to be able to form a working relationship then it's better to know sooner rather than later.

You also need to prepare and rehearse your pitch. You've only got fifteen minutes, so you need to make them count. Be positive and confident. Just like potential life-partners, clients can smell desperation.

On a practical level, make sure you know where the meeting is taking place and minimize logistical stress on the day by working out in advance how you will get there and when you need to set out. If you are driving, make sure you know where you can park. Most importantly, do not be late.

LOOKING THE PART

As with any work you do, as well as being prepared for the meeting it's also important that you look the part in terms of both body language and dress code.

Some years ago a colleague of mine with an impeccable track record in his career working in top companies at a high level went to interview for a senior head office role. Having come from a corporate background, he was tempted to put on his best suit as that's how he'd usually go to interviews, but as this one was at a well-known high-street retailer, he thought he'd dress in items from their clothing range. Unsurprisingly, most of the other candidates wore suits. He was offered the job, and was told that one of the reasons he'd been chosen was that it seemed as though he already worked there, so they knew he'd fit in.

If you are working in a new sector then do some research before you go to meet a client. It's amazing how much your appearance and comportment can affect the impression you make. Many years ago I worked for a production company budgeting programme ideas for older and more experienced producers. As I was younger than them, I made a conscious effort to dress a little more smartly than they did and act confidently. It paid off. One of the producers I was working with said, 'I always believe what you say because you look like you know what you're talking about.'

If you work in more than one sector then you may need to vary your appearance to suit different clients. A meeting with a professional services organization will demand a suit whereas a meeting with a small charity is likely to be far less formal.

LISTENING

When you are in a client meeting you won't learn anything by listening to yourself talk. Of course, you need to do your pitch and introduce yourself, but after that make the effort to be quiet and listen. *You can sell more through listening than through speaking*. The client has a problem that they think you can solve, so listen carefully to what the problem is. You are listening to gain from the client information about:

- what is important to them and what their values are;
- what is missing; what they think they want and need to solve their problem.

Resist the temptation to interrupt or rebut the client. Just keep listening, and whilst you are doing so start thinking about solutions that you can offer.

You can create great empathy simply by making someone feel heard. When they've finished explaining their challenges, follow up with confirmatory statements that both reinforce the fact that you were listening and add clarification to any uncertain areas.

Clarification statements start with something like, 'So, what I am hearing is . . .' Or, 'Can you help me to understand more about . . .' These allow you to qualify what you have heard and start to frame the conversation in the direction you want it to go. Don't be afraid of silence.

As a listener, your aim is to be an enabler, so make sure the language you use when you do speak is enabling. If you can remove one word from your vocabulary, make it the word 'but'. But stops a conversation dead. But challenges the speaker. 'But' is usually the start of a sentence that continues 'the problem with that is . . .'

That's not an enabling way of conversing. It's challenging your client and can be seen as undermining them.

Use 'and' instead. And connects you to the client. And enables the discussion.

By really listening you can appreciate the challenges from the client's perspective as opposed to your own interpretation of what they might want. It can only be a winning strategy.

Don't underestimate how hard proper listening is. Try it out on your friends and family. Start a conversation, ask them about their day, their work, or what they think of current events. Take the time to really listen to them. Your old habits will try to kick in. You'll want to rebut the conversation and join in. You'll start to zone out and think about what you want to eat or check on your phone. Work through this. Don't let other thoughts distract you. Keep listening. And then when they've finished, respond with a clarification statement.

After you've tried it out, reflect on how the conversation went for you and for them. Ask for feedback – you may or may not have told whoever you're talking to that you are trying out your listening skills. Either way the response will be useful. And if you really want to test your listening skills, try having a conversation about politics with someone who holds an opposing view to your own.

RECOGNIZING BUYING SIGNALS

The most important thing to recognize when you are selling is how to identify when a customer is giving off *buying signals*. People often ask me how I can tell if a client is interested in my services. I know because I'm listening for their buying signals. Some clients are more obvious than others, but if you know what to listen for then they are easy to spot.

It can be a change in language from the client, pushing you on what you can do for them, to the client trying to sell themselves to you. If you've ever been interviewed for a job and been successful, then you'll probably recognize that moment when the interviewer stops interviewing you and starts selling the company to you. That is a buying signal.

An example which demonstrates this point well is this one from Percy Emmett. He trained me to be a facilitator delivering the Nesta Creative Enterprise Toolkit and is someone I really admire.

Imagine you run a small company producing pens. You land a meeting with one of the largest pen retailers in the country – which is a huge opportunity. You come out of the meeting and give me a call to report on the meeting and this is what the retailer said to you:

- I like your pens.
- I think they will sit well in our portfolio of products.
- I think our customers will buy them.
- But I just don't have time to deal with this at the moment.

The question now is: what was the outcome of the meeting? Did it go well? Did you sell any pens?

The majority of people on hearing this will say no. The meeting was no good. It was a waste of a morning. They didn't have time for you. You'll have to find another customer (even though they are the largest in the country).

But look back again at what was said. The first three statements were completely positive.

✓ I like your pens.
✓ I think they will sit well in our portfolio of products.
✓ I think our customers will buy them.

They like the pens. Not only that but they will sit well in their portfolio of products and, most importantly of all, they think their customers will buy them. What part of that are not buying signals? They really *do* want to buy the pens.

Then comes the dreaded 'but':

✗ But I just don't have time to deal with this at the moment.

A 'but' at this point in the conversation makes our brains hear 'no deal'. But that's not what has been said. At this point you have no idea what this but means. A lack of time yes. But in what way?

Perhaps they are just back from holiday and were desperate to meet with you but need a week to catch up. Perhaps there are operational issues which mean that the way you are presenting the pens doesn't work for them. Perhaps, perhaps, perhaps. You need to find out.

The way to proceed is to focus on how you can solve their problem of time scarcity. Because if you can solve that, then it's very likely that a sale is on the table. You are a small company; they are a large one. You have the opportunity and almost certainly the capability to reshape your operations in order to deliver product to them.

I find this example very powerful because it shows that, by taking the time to listen and understand your client's problems, you can mould your services to fit their needs better.

THE FIRST MEETING

Let's assume your meeting has come about from one of your four-line emails. It's going to be a short discussion, so you want to gather as much information as quickly as possible. You've already qualified who you are in your email, and it's reasonable to assume that the client has bought into your credibility or you wouldn't have been invited, so now it's about you assessing where the pain is for them.

Take notes and empathize. Use encouraging statements such as 'That's really interesting . . .' You are looking for where they have pain or problems that you can solve for them with your services. As it's only a brief meeting, don't waste time on negotiations. Instead you can wrap up by saying, 'I'll get a proposal and some costs over to you by the end of the week.'

Remember, this was your first date, and not all first dates end with a goodbye kiss. If you come away feeling that the client doesn't share your values or value your work, move on. If they start to make things difficult for you, move on.

If the meeting went well, then the proposal that you put together should reflect this early stage in your relationship. Make a modest request, something that you believe the person you met with can easily sign off on. It's very tempting to try to sell a client too much, too quickly, especially if you've had a great meeting and you can see there is plenty of work you could do. However, less is more. Start by gaining their trust with a small piece of work and upsell after that.

That first meeting is an exploratory one for both parties. *You don't have to provide an answer to the client there and then.* You are being brought in to support a company and a client because of your expertise and your capability. Don't be pushed into coming up with an off-the-cuff answer or a throwaway price – if you need to go away and think about it then do just that. This can be one of the hardest things to do, particularly if the sales process is very new to you, but the client will usually respect you more if you follow up the meeting in writing with a formal proposal in which you have taken the time to consider their specific needs before quoting. Remember that, even if this is a task you perform day in, day out for many different people, so far as the client is concerned it is work you are doing solely for them and their brand, so treat it as such.

One mentor of mine – a senior media executive – used to go by the mantra 'If you need an answer today then the answer is always no'. He utilized this with great success inside corporations and boardrooms, and it is worth thinking about how and when you could apply this strategy.

READING THE ROOM

When you are in a meeting room with a client or clients then, as well as pitching yourself and your services, and actively listening to what is being said, you need to be reading the room. That means reading the body language, posture and expressions of everyone present to gauge their level of interest in the discussion.

Someone who is leaning back with arms crossed and looking out of the window is not showing huge signs of engagement, whereas someone leaning in towards the discussion and following it intently is actively taking part, even if they aren't speaking.

Recall the decision-maker analysis from Chapter 3. When you are in the meeting you want to be working out who in the room are the influencers and, most importantly, who is the decision maker. If you are working with a big organization there may be many people around the table, so this can be quite a challenge.

Of course, if the decision maker is not there you are not going to make a sale that day, so concentrate instead on the influencers who will be your sponsors after the meeting. It's important to understand very quickly the role of everyone in the room and focus your pitch and attention accordingly.

For example, an influencer is likely to want to know additional technical knowledge about the work you do so that they can be best informed for their influencing, whereas a decision maker will be assessing what benefit you can bring to the company. Does your proposal fit with their strategy and is the cost right?

Doing all this on your own is hard work, but becomes easier with practice and experience.

Although in theory you are selling your services to a company, in practice you are selling yourself to one or more people. Those people have lives and families, just like you. They want to perform well and make the best decisions they can using the knowledge they are given by you. So it's up to you to ensure that you deliver, get through to them and don't waste their time.

The dynamics of the meetings will differ depending on the size of the organization you are pitching to. A meeting with a big institution will usually involve several people, so will take longer to set up as more diaries need to be consulted. On the flipside, a small organization that doesn't often work with freelancers might roll out the red carpet for a meeting and make a quite enjoyable fuss about having you visit them.

Whatever scenario you find yourself in you will be faced with the same challenges. Is the decision maker in the room? And do they like what you are saying? If you can come out of the meeting having answered only those two questions, you will have done a great job.

CONCLUDE THE MEETING WITH ACTIONS

A meeting is only as valuable as the actions that result from it. Make sure you are clear on the action points that emerge from the discussion and who is going to do them. It's good practice to wrap up any meeting with a quick run-through of the actions to reinforce the next steps. This has the added benefit of making people feel positive about the meeting, what has been achieved and what the next steps are.

The most likely result is that you commit to doing something, such as preparing a proposal, so make sure you communicate clearly what you will do by when and then stick to your timeline. I'll often add an extra few days' leeway to ensure I can get it done by the deadline I've given. This means that I can still meet it even if unexpected issues crop up, and if they don't then I'm in a position to deliver early, which signals added commitment to the client.

FOLLOWING UP

After any meeting you should immediately drop a quick thank-you email to the client to thank them for their time, remind them of any salient points from the meeting that you think they need reminding of and set out your next steps with a timeline of what you will do by when. In this way you are keeping control of the conversation whilst you put your full proposal together.

PREPARING YOUR PROPOSAL

A proposal is a written outline of the work that you plan to deliver for that client. They vary in length and detail, usually in proportion to the size and scale of the job. If your proposal is responding to a brief, then make sure you reflect what the brief asked for. And if you feel the brief is scant and not fully formed then your proposal is an opportunity to flesh this out.

A good proposal should tell the client everything they need to know to make a decision on whether to buy your services, particularly the value they will bring. Back in Chapter 6 you drew up a proposal template with a boilerplate copy. Now is the time to fill in the meat of the proposal with the specific detail of the work you have discussed during the meeting.

You've probably heard the phrase 'never assume – it makes an ass out of u and me'. If you've made assumptions in your proposal or pitch then make sure you identify these clearly and up front.

If pitching for project work, for example a client wants to contract you for a number of days over a fixed period of time (e.g. ten days over three months), be aware that this has the most potential for misquoting and misjudging by freelancer and client alike. The key to managing successful project work is to ensure that you and the client are clear from the outset what you have agreed. For a small project this can be as simple as writing down in an email:

- what it is you are expecting to do;
- what is to be delivered (e.g. video, report, presentation, training sessions);
- over what time period;
- how much you will be paid.

Ensure you are both clear about what you are going to do and that you have a 'meeting of the minds'. Leaving things in the grey murky area will only lead to confusion and misunderstandings at a later date – just at the point when you are either about to be paid or when you are thinking it might be a good time to talk about the next project you could do. Not a time you want confusion rearing its head.

For a larger project, a more detailed approach is to think of the project in terms of SMART targets, by which I mean Specific, Measurable, Agreed, Realistic and Timebound targets. And if this detail hasn't come from the client already, then sending them a proposal detailing within it SMART targets that you can identify can be helpful for all.

- **Specific** targets include the key details concerning what the project is about, who/what needs to be achieved for the project etc.
- **Measurable** targets for project work include your estimates of the number of days for each specific aspect of the project, measurable outcomes etc.
- **Agreed** targets are key touch points in the project where you and the client can review progress and ensure that the project is on track. It can be as simple as regular review point meetings, or an update email that keeps the client on board and in agreement with the progress of the project.
- **Realistic** targets are those you can reasonably be expected to achieve: you are hired to be a freelancer, not a superhero.
- **Timebound** targets are the deadlines for key aspects of the project, e.g. a specific completion date, midpoint review or presentation.

Take the time to pull together this detail at the start of the project and you will have an agreed framework that you and your client can refer to throughout. That way if project creep rears its head, your framework will be in place to reopen discussions with the client and agree a way forward. It doesn't matter what the outcome is, the point here is that you and the client have a clear framework of what you need to achieve because of the proposal you have drawn up.

I'm often asked in workshops why the freelancer should put so much unpaid time and effort into preparing a proposal when it might not be accepted. Why can't the client prepare it? To me, the answer is simple. The client is hiring you for one of two reasons: either for your specific expertise or because they need an extra resource in their team. If it's the former then they won't know your area well enough to assess what a good proposal for your work looks like, therefore you need to write it. If the latter, then the chances are they are too busy and the proposal won't get written. Either way, if you want the work you need to write the proposal.

Remember, your first proposal for a new client will be for something modest, so focus it this way. You can refer to a bigger vision as part of the proposal, but make sure it is clear you are only trying to sell them this first small step of the larger vision for now.

PRICING YOUR PROPOSAL

As well as outlining the scope of the project for the client you will need to provide a cost for you to deliver the work. We looked at rate determination and variation in Chapter 5. It's now that you'll need to decide what rate you think is appropriate for this proposal.

The overall price will include the costs of any equipment, other freelancers or consumables you will need to source as part of the project outline. Remember that when pricing a project you should include all the *actual* costs of delivering your services. Just because you own the specialist equipment necessary to deliver your services doesn't mean the client shouldn't pay for it when you use it to deliver their work, so make sure you include costs that reflect this usage (such as a daily hire charge for your equipment). Whatever your project is, be clear what is and what isn't included in your quote.

Clients don't like the nasty surprise of an unexpected extra cost being tacked on at the end of a project. And it will never be their fault: remember, it's your reputation at stake. If things are unclear to you then they are likely to be unclear to your client as well. Don't hide from the grey murky areas but embrace ways of finding clarity in them – you are likely to be solving a problem for the client by doing so.

It's highly likely that your clients will want to negotiate on your price, especially if you've quoted at the sharp-intake-of-breath level, so make sure you've allowed a margin of 10–15 per cent in your pricing so you can be bartered down a little.

DISCOUNTING AS A STRATEGY

You may rightly have inferred by now that I like to charge like a wounded elephant when it comes to pricing. But believe it or not I do still find room for discounting as a pricing strategy. Yes, you did read that right, I used the 'd' word.

But if you've learned anything so far, you'll suspect there is going to be a catch to my version of discounting. And you are right. There is a catch and in fact I should probably have called this section 'Discounting (But Not Really)'. This pricing strategy works best when you are quoting for your services to deliver a big project for a new client. As part of your proposal you'll draw up a detailed budget of all the stages in the planning, execution and wrap-up. And you'll cost in your time plus equipment and expenses to deliver. You'll charge your time at full market rates for the number of days required. Then you'll look at the total and say to yourself, 'I'll never win this new client pricing at this level. I'll have to reduce my costs and rates.' The chances are that by the time you are at this stage in the quoting and pitching process, you will have an idea of what you think the new client might pay.

Rather than reducing your daily rate throughout, reducing the number of days and reducing the equipment costs (especially any that you already own), I prefer a more strategic approach based on what I think the client might pay.

I start by preparing a summary sheet of the costs for the client with this top-end price forming the basis of the quote but offering in a line that says 'new client introductory discount' and takes a percentage off. I use this percentage rate to discount the total cost to the level that I think the client will pay, including the sharp intake of breath. Before I submit my proposal, though, I do double check that I really can, *and am happy to*, deliver the work at this reduced price.

This strategy is most successful when the discount applied is at least 15 per cent. Anything less than that doesn't look like a special price to the client. If your discount is less than 15 per cent go back and redo your sums so that the final price including the discount remains at the same level – this will mean you will need to put *up* the original figures.

The effect of this strategy is twofold. First, you've already offered the client a substantial discount, so it's not easy for them to negotiate further. Second, it signals to the client what the real cost of the job should be. This means that, should they want further work from you, there is a built-in mechanism for you to increase the price. You've already said on the first quote submitted that this is a 'new client introductory discount'. That doesn't apply to subsequent jobs. By hiring your services for the first job they have implicitly agreed with your proposal. True, you won't always be able to increase the fee for subsequent jobs to the undiscounted price, but theoretically you've made Job 1 at worst break-even, so any future work at a higher rate should be more profitable.

VALIDITY PERIOD FOR YOUR QUOTE

'Prices quoted are valid for thirty days'. It's a simple enough statement. It's written on pretty much every quote you ever receive. On the surface it does mean that you can change the price if the client doesn't confirm within thirty days. That's great, since it gives you flexibility to adapt your pricing in the future.

However, there is a much more powerful opportunity at play here. If the client hasn't responded to you when the thirty days are up (you'll need to track this on your prospect list), you can send them a polite reminder that their old quote has expired and attach a new one, also valid for thirty days. It's remarkable how many times the client will come back to you with an apology, saying they've been busy, thanking you for the reminder and giving you the go-ahead.

THE SMALL PRINT

You should *always quote in writing*, even if it's just an email, stating what you are going to do, by when and for how much. This helps avoid misunderstandings and prevents arguments later. Legally, this is called an 'offer'.

When the client accepts your offer and agrees to pay the price you've quoted (the payment is called a 'consideration' legally), a contract exists. When you supply the product or service as set out in your offer, the client has to pay you.

Your terms and conditions of business should be on every proposal and every invoice you send. Whilst your proposal details the bespoke part of your work, what your client can expect from you (the services) and what you expect from them; you also need to add the terms and conditions common to every job – how and when you expect to be paid for the services, what will happen if payment is late, title and risk if goods are being supplied, who owns any intellectual property and how long the quote is valid for.

There are plenty of resources out there to help you with this, including trade associations and professional bodies. Just remember to state clearly and unambiguously what the agreement is between you and the client, and ensure it is understood by both parties *before* the contract begins. (If you find yourself reaching for your terms and conditions and quoting these to a client after that point, then the relationship has almost certainly broken down.)

CHECK EVERYTHING

Now that you've pulled your proposal together for your client, with associated costs, you are ready to proofread it from beginning to end. And I mean really scrutinize it. Every. Single. Word. And. Number.

It's frightening how many small errors you'll find when you really look. If your client spots these it's not going to create the impression you're after. Once you are happy that your proposal is checked you can save it as a PDF and submit it.

Your first sale is gathering momentum.

10.

WINNING YOUR FIRST CUSTOMER

You've got an interested customer. They've read your proposal and invited you in for a second meeting. Now it's time to reel them in, negotiate and close the deal. But first there is some more pre-meeting prep to do.

PRE-MEETING PREP

You'll need to undertake further research on your client and the sector they work in to see what other challenges they are facing. If you can find a way to articulate how your services also help to solve any wider issues it will increase your credibility and might open the door to the broader sector.

You'll also need to prepare your detailed pitch, which this time will be a longer presentation covering your proposal, with time allowed for the client to ask questions. Again, rehearse before the meeting. If you are doing a presentation, make sure you have all the tech and cables you need and that everything is fully charged and ready to go.

Keep listening out for alarm bells as you do your prep. The more potential pitfalls you can be aware of in advance, the better you can focus your pitch to ensure you minimize the risk of them becoming an issue.

Be prepared to negotiate. Negotiating is all about understanding the dynamic between yourself and your client, *knowing your value to them* and – crucially – being able to articulate it. You want your clients to value the work you do. By value, I don't mean how much you charge, I mean *the value you add* to your customer's business by doing that voodoo that you do so well. Knowing your value in the marketplace and the value you add to a particular project defines your margin for negotiation with the client.

I do like a bit of a negotiation when I book in a freelancer to help me with a project. I want them to think, 'OK, there is a deal to be made here, but there's a little work to be done on price, as it's more expensive than I thought it would be.' That way, as the buyer, I feel like I've got a bit of a bargain. If I bite your hand off straight away for your quote with no quibbles, it's likely there was room for me to pay more.

You should also decide beforehand what your 'walk away' price is: at what point will you walk away from the work because the price is too low? Just as the client will have an idea of the value your participation offers to them, you need to assess the value of this work to you. Make sure you leave room for manoeuvre in any price conversation.

THE SECOND MEETING

This second meeting should be the one that tells you how serious the client is and whether your proposal will be accepted. This is the all-important stage, so once you've delivered your pitch and heard their questions, read the room and qualify the client. By this I mean satisfy yourself that the client meets the following criteria:

1. They **need** your services.
2. They have a **budget** for your services.
3. They want your services **now.**

Assuming they fulfil all three criteria, then you should aim to close the sale at this meeting.

Just as during the first meeting, you'll need all your wits about you – pitching, listening, reading the room and looking out for the all-important buying signals. Assuming you spot those, you have an opportunity to close the deal.

ABC: ALWAYS BE CLOSING

There are four main techniques for closing a sale:

- The 'fear close'.
- The 'alternative close'.
- The 'outcome-based close'.
- The 'silent close'.

The classic type of 'fear close' is 'buy now while stocks last' or 'sale must end soon', but if you've ever bought an electronic item, you'll have had a different type of 'fear close' used on you. You know the moment. You've picked the machine that you want to purchase and you've gone to the counter to pay for it and suddenly the sales person is offering to sell you a whole range of additional guarantees in case it goes wrong. They are putting the fear of the machine breaking down some time in the future into your head to scare you into parting with more cash now. The salesperson no doubt earns commission and the company makes a healthy profit on this extra sale.

The problem with the fear close is that it doesn't set up your relationship with the client in a way that is sustainable in the long term. It feels like a trick to make extra money, even when it's a genuine proposition. You don't want your client to feel that way about you, so it's probably best avoided as an obvious tactic. But you might hint that you're really busy at the moment and expecting offers of work at any time . . .

The 'alternative close' is used when the item you really want is out of stock and an attempt is made to sell you something else instead. It's a favourite in shoe shops when you ask to try on a pair of shoes they don't have in stock in your size, so they offer you two or more alternatives to choose from. If a client asks if you can provide something you don't have, try saying, 'No, but I can offer you either X or Y. Which would you prefer?'

Another variation on this is 'Do you want it in red or blue?' – the principle here is that you're taking it for granted that the customer is going to buy, it's just the colour, flavour or whatever that needs deciding upon. This is a very different proposition from 'Do you want it or not?' The alternative close is something that can be built into your client proposal as a set of options. As an aside, this close works really well on toddlers too!

The close I tend to use the most is the 'outcome-based close'. This is when you sell the client the results or outcomes that they want to achieve. Remember the women selling their video production services to schools? They learned to sell using this close and the schools started to buy.

Earlier I used the example that people buy a drill because they need holes, not a drill, so will buy whatever gives them better, faster, neater holes. With outcome-based selling you take this one step further by adding a reward to the benefit. For example the better, faster, neater holes can be used to double the buyer's storage space with shelving they've been putting off erecting and they can then get to the pub sooner.

This type of selling centres around customer-focussed thinking and articulating why your customer should choose you, so is likely to be the one you will use most often.

The final tactic to employ when closing a deal, and one that works well in combination with the above, is the 'silent close'.

Say you are discussing your proposal with the client and you finish the discussion with, 'So I'll do that for £X.' And then you stay silent and wait for the client to speak. There are only three possible responses:

- 'Yes – well, that's great you've got the deal.' Hooray! Thank them and **stop selling** – don't lose it again by starting to talk and trying to sell them some more. They've bought already.
- 'No, I can't agree to that.' Don't despair. Ask what the reason is. It shouldn't be that you are too expensive as you are only selling them something modest.
- 'Hmm. Maybe we could work something out.' That's a buying signal. Probe them further. Listen. Ask them what still needs to happen and when they might be able to get an answer and say you'll follow up with them again at that time.

You will get a lot of maybes and you will need to keep on top of them. Nudge them regularly but nicely. Some will turn into sales and some will turn into time wasters. Your CRM software can help you do the heavy lifting on this as long as you keep it up to date.

DISTRESS PURCHASES

A distress purchase is one where a client needs something desperately and urgently – usually immediately – that hasn't been planned for or envisaged. A domestic example might be that your boiler has broken down on the coldest night of the year or your drain is blocked and you have a garden full of sewage. Fixing something like that is a distress purchase. There's no time to shop around or haggle, you just need it doing right now, and you'll be prepared to pay a premium to get it done.

Getting a distressed client out of a hole when they've been let down or something has gone wrong can reap huge rewards in terms of loyalty. When a company is looking to hire a new freelancer as a distress purchase it's usually because either they have no existing contacts in this field or their go-to people are busy. It's an opportunity for you to put your skills to work for a client you might not have otherwise had the opportunity to work with, so make the most of it.

GET IT IN WRITING

You have just received your first 'Yes' from a client and shaken hands on a deal. Fantastic! Well done. It's time to pat yourself on the back and give a cheer. You have proved that you can sell yourself. Your freelance career is gaining traction.

Before you crack on and get started, however, you need to make sure you have that 'Yes' confirmed **in writing** and in accordance with the client's purchasing, procurement or ordering systems. (They will have small print too.)

The first time you work with any client you will need to be set up as an authorized supplier on their systems, in particular their finance systems (otherwise you won't get paid), so expect some forms to fill in. Make sure you are the professional freelancer who gets on with filling in this paperwork as soon as it is sent, not the sort who has to be chased for it. In general, the larger the company, the more complex this process will be. A large public-sector organization is likely to have several layers of bureaucracy; a small company hiring few freelancers will have a much simpler system and might not even ask for information like this up front.

Once you are an authorized supplier, you should receive a contract or purchase order setting out the services you will provide. The exact payment schedule and terms will vary according to circumstances. If it is a chunky project over a long period you might be paid a percentage on signature, a percentage after a midpoint review or milestone and a final percentage on delivery. This is your opportunity to discuss the terms with the client and make sure they work for you.

One freelancer I mentored told me how she couldn't afford to keep working for one of her clients. The work they gave her was great and money was good, but she nearly went broke as they would pay nothing until thirty days after the project was completed, which meant she had to keep enough in the bank to cover all her household costs for up to four months. She didn't realize this wasn't standard practice, and that she could negotiate payment terms with the client, which she did successfully on the next occasion.

When you receive a contract for your services from your client make sure you *read it thoroughly* to ensure you are clear about what you are signing up for and under what terms. It should state clearly any deadlines, the work to be done and the payments to be made. If you will incur expenses whilst you are doing the work, make sure there is a provision for you to claim these back. Take note of any exclusivity or intellectual property clauses that might limit other work you can do.

Again, don't delay returning the contract. The client wants you to do the work, you want to do the work, so you need to deal swiftly with whatever processes lie between your client saying yes and you getting started. As soon as you are happy with the wording, sign the contract and get on with the work.

ON A PROMISE

In the euphoria of winning your first customer, it's important not to lose sight of the fact that the *long-term value of every client* is vital. You need to *build solid relationships* with them so that they want to keep working with you.

When you commit to doing a piece of work for a client you make a promise to them. Your expertise has enabled you to make that promise; now you must demonstrate your integrity by keeping it.

Clients buy your services not only because they have a need for them but also because they have bought into *you* as the person who can fulfil that need. Make sure you deliver on that promise every time. That will ensure you build solid, long-term client relationships.

11.

PREPARING FOR WORK

Closing your first sale is an exciting moment, so enjoy it and be proud of yourself. But before you get started on your first contract, take a moment to check your work environment and make sure it is set up in the best way for you.

PREPARING YOUR WORK ENVIRONMENT

Think about how and where you like to work. If you're home based, there is no one telling you where your desk should be. It's your choice where you put it – by the radiator, with a window view or in the summer house. What type of environment has been most productive for you in the past? What in particular made it good for you? Conversely, think about any factors that have ever made you less effective. I freelanced in one company that had very nice-looking glass desks, but my hands and fingers got so cold in the winter that I couldn't type. I had to endure it as the project required me to be on-site quite regularly, but I can assure you I shall never buy a glass desk for my own use.

One thing I did take away from being in an office environment was the importance of having a proper office chair that supports my back and is the right height. I know that I will be sitting in it for extended periods and it is my responsibility and no one else's to look after my health and safety at work. I also like to use a good desk lamp that casts a pool of light over my working area but doesn't create glare.

As you prepare your working area, it's up to you to arrange it how you want it. It's worth putting some thought into what makes a good working space for you. Does having a window to look directly out of inspire or distract you? Is the temperature comfortable? Is the lighting right? If anyone else will be sharing your space, either permanently or as a visitor, are they adequately provided for?

SETTING UP YOUR DESK

Irrespective of speciality, most freelancers make use of a desk at least some of the time, so it's an important tool of the trade. Now that you've got yours in the right place it's time to furnish it with what you need. The first item is usually your computer. This is your trusty steed. You need to be able to depend on it, so make sure you have a machine that is reliable and up to the job. The last thing you want as you embark on your first commission is to be worrying that your IT will let you down.

One of the best things I ever did was turn my laptop into a PC for working at home. I did this by buying a computer monitor, a keyboard and a mouse, so I could sit at my desk with a large screen, plug in my laptop and use it like a desktop computer. Then, whenever I go to a meeting, I just take the laptop with me and I have all my files to hand.

I learned the hard way that having two power cables for your laptop is essential with this setup. Keep one at your desk and one in your work bag – otherwise you'll find yourself about to give a presentation and your laptop dies or, my personal favourite, you arrive home on a Friday night with a dead laptop and a weekend's work to do, only to discover you've left the cable behind and can't retrieve it until Monday morning.

You should also look at what software you need to do your work and have in place a reliable recovery solution, such as an external hard drive or cloud storage, so if your machine does give up the ghost – and it will – at least you know that all your hard work is safe. Cloud storage has the benefit of being able to offer instant back-up, and is my preferred option. I also have a printer nearby (again, I'm old school and I like to print out some documents to read).

Away from IT, you'll want some pens and a decent notepad or notebook – somewhere, anyway, to write your to-do lists, make notes during calls and use whilst at meetings. (I know lots of people use a tablet to do this these days; I've tried, but it's just not for me.)

My mobile phone is my lifeline, and always close to hand. It keeps me in touch with my clients and up to date with what's happening. Just like your computer, your mobile must be up to the job, with good battery life (or a juice pack), email and internet access and the ability to open documents in cloud storage.

If, like me, you are combining home and family life with working, your mobile allows you to keep it all going whilst still doing the school run. I'm not claiming to be a super-mum – far from it, I have great childcare and plenty of it or our house wouldn't function – but I know my boys do like me to do the school run a few times a week, so I work hard to build that into my schedule. It's easy in the quiet times and much harder when it's busy. What I do know is that I can keep an awful lot happening just with my mobile in my pocket and none of my clients are any the wiser that I'm also enjoying some family time.

REMOTE WORKING

Developments in technology mean that the opportunities for freelance working have changed dramatically in recent years. Technology enables people to be connected even though they are not in the same office, and remote working has increased significantly as a result. You can be down the road or in another city, country or even continent. That's not to say working remotely doesn't have its issues, but provided you know what they are you can plan for them and can make it work for you.

The challenges of remote working fall into two areas:

- How you stay connected with your clients.
- How you stay happy and healthy.

STAYING CONNECTED WITH CLIENTS

Maintaining good connections with your clients is predominantly about communications and building and maintaining their trust. They need to have confidence that you are doing what you have been contracted to do. The required level of communication will depend on the type of work you are doing. This is something you can address in your original proposal.

If I am working on a strategy project, doing research and interviewing people, I might have contact with the client only at monthly review meetings, when I'll give a progress update and discuss next steps. If I am working as a producer on a live film event, however, I'll often be in daily contact with the client.

These two extremes throw up differing challenges for remote working. The producing work is very operational and I need to be across it constantly. Even if it's not a full-time contract, the client will expect me to respond in a timely fashion. I try to avoid commitments to work on specific projects at specific times so that I can arrange my own hours and prioritize my work to suit. Even though I'm usually working from home I rarely feel alone or isolated as there is plenty of interaction, both by email and on the telephone, which makes me feel connected and part of a team.

Working remotely means that I send many more emails asking quick questions than I would do working in an office, where I'd find out answers by walking about and talking to people.

From the client's perspective, they want to be confident that I am getting on with the work that needs doing so I make sure to keep them updated and arrange regular check-in calls as well to go through details. The client has to trust me to carry on unsupervised and deliver the work at the level they want.

Today, potential clients can see from my experience that I can be trusted to do the work. Their leap of faith is to be sure that I will get on with it when I am not in their office where they can keep an eye on me.

When I first started my career, working from home had a dreadful reputation. People would joke around the office that X was 'working from home today' as a euphemism for skiving off, and in the absence of email and mobile phones people really did go off the radar when they left the building. You didn't know whether they were working or not. Also they rarely had access at home to the resources we do today.

Even today, trust can still be hard to build, particularly when clients are less used to the work being carried out remotely. With these types of project I'll work extra hard to make sure my communications are frequent and my clients are always up to speed. Whilst keeping clients in the loop can be hard work to start with, once you have gained their trust they can be your most loyal customers.

STAYING HAPPY AND HEALTHY

The strategy consultations I do as a remote worker are a wholly different ballgame. These are very much research-based projects that involve initial consultation and research and then putting together a report and presentation. Once the client has commissioned the work, I am left to get on with it. They don't expect or want daily check-in emails or calls. They've often hired me because they don't have time to do the work themselves, in which case they really don't want to hear from me every five minutes. The project usually starts with an initial meeting to go through the brief, agree a plan of action for the consultation and set a date for the next meeting, when I'll update them on progress.

Such work can be very isolating, so I need to manage my own well-being especially carefully. There isn't the constant email and phone chatter of production work. It can be slow to get started as the research consultations can take time to set up. Then there is a busy period out and about doing the consultations. Then it's back to my desk to pull together all I've gathered into a report and presentation. Aside from the periodic check-in meetings with the client, I am working by myself. On the one hand, it's great; the client trusts that I can do the work and lets me get on with it. On the other hand, working in isolation means I can easily become distracted when things get challenging. At such times I'll often move to a co-working space for a part of the week. Here there are fewer distractions than at home, plus I'm in an environment with other remote workers. I get some conversation and interaction making tea and over lunch to mitigate the isolation, and then it's back to it, with everyone getting on with their own work. There's nothing like a room full of busy people to motivate you to get your head down.

For me, the right co-working space can be hugely productive. It's a place where I can focus on what I'm doing with maximum concentration and thought. There's little else to do, so little to distract me. Find a space to suit the work you are doing. Many offer flexible terms that allow you to drop in and out as required. If you're ever feeling isolated, give it a try.

As an extrovert and a freelance working mum, co-working has been a life-saver for me, particularly when my kids were small. Before I discovered it there would be days when I'd drop them off at nursery and go back to my desk at home. I'd realize by mid-afternoon that I'd not had a conversation with an adult all day and then I'd be off to pick them up again. Co-working changed all that. I don't need much interaction, just someone to shoot the breeze with, offer a cup of tea to and feel acknowledged by as a working adult rather than a parent. It makes me feel part of the world and not stuck in a bubble.

A quick and easy fix to feeling isolated is to pick up your laptop and go for a coffee. Cafés are somewhere you can feel connected with the world around you as well as to the online world. You have to decide what works best for you, and I expect you'll find different solutions at different phases in your work.

That's the beauty of freelancing – you can keep what's best for you when it works and drop it when it doesn't. The trick is to be aware when something is having a negative impact on your life so that you can make a change. Because you can.

12.

DELIVERING YOUR FIRST PIECE OF WORK

This is the moment you've been building up to. It's your first opportunity to do the work that you became a freelancer to do.

Successful freelancers keep their promises by doing what they say they are going to do, when they say they are going to do it, and they do it well. Your reputation is all; if you are seen as a safe pair of hands who is easy and pleasant to deal with, the work – and the money – should follow.

But to establish your reputation with this first client you need to show them not only *how well you can do the work* but *how brilliant you are to collaborate with* through the entire process, which means establishing clear lines of communication and managing their expectations.

CLEAR COMMUNICATIONS

Checking in with the client, especially a new client, from the outset about how they like to be kept updated and how often is a smart way to start. It reassures your client that you are putting their needs first and it gives you valuable intelligence on how to keep them happy.

Flapping and panicking in their direction is not going to inspire confidence. If a challenge arises then know when it's appropriate to refer up. When you do refer up, provide your client with a selection of carefully considered solutions that you can discuss in order to plan a solution. Be sensitive to the best mode of communication for the situation – you might send an email to flag a challenge but follow that up with a phone call or meeting.

MANAGING EXPECTATIONS

There are tactics and strategies you can employ to manage a client's expectations, the first of which is to set yourself realistic time frames in which to do the work, or even just the next part of it. The SMART targets in your proposal (page 184) should address this.

It all goes back to trust. If you make clear when you can deliver something by and then deliver it on time, you will build the client's trust and they will expect that what you *say* you will do you *will* do.

A healthy respect for deadlines is a must if you are going to manage your client's expectations. And if for any reason you can't meet the agreed deadline then communicate that as soon as you can. Don't just watch it sail past whilst you hide under the duvet with your phone on silent.

Although the client may be annoyed by your late delivery it will be as nothing compared with their anger should you miss the deadline unannounced. Your work may be just a small part of your client's larger project and you probably have no idea of the knock-on effects if you let them down. At least if you tell them early it is usually possible to find a solution that works for both of you.

Being clear about the boundaries of the work you do can also be important in managing a client's expectations. If the client doesn't know much about the work you do, they might expect too much of you. This happens with my producing work. I'll sometimes be asked to discuss with a potential new client a film they want to make, and at the meeting I explain that I work with a team, that I don't do the filming or the editing but bring specialists in for that. I can see quickly if the person they want for the job is not me but a multi-skilled operator. That isn't something I will ever be, but I know quite a number so I'll introduce them.

I know digital marketers who say similar things. They can take care of the overall strategy but their boundaries are they don't do the day-to-day social posting. They add more value to the client with their strategy work. In their view, the day-to-day social media posting is operational and should be taken on by the client, or they can recommend another freelancer.

FINISH THE JOB

The best way to manage your client's expectations is to finish the job on time and on budget and to do it well. And by finish the job I mean all of it, including any final paperwork.

I've seen freelancers who are very good at the main aspects of their work but let themselves down by not completing the job fully – they are very pleasant when chased but they are now 'so busy on another project' and will 'get to it next week' and so on. But next week never comes.

Clearly, they don't understand the value to the client of tying up all the loose ends. Projects, especially those funded with public money, often have important paperwork deliverables that measure their outcomes. If you don't deliver that for the client then you could be jeopardizing their ability to submit their report. Don't be that person, because after a while, however brilliantly you fulfil the main part of the project, your clients will move on to other freelancers since you just aren't delivering to their needs.

GOING NATIVE

It's easy to become wrapped up in the work you are doing, getting too close to it and losing sight of who's paying the bill. Whilst on the one hand that is commendable because you are putting in a great deal of effort, on the other hand the client paying the bill may not feel that you are spending your time and their money wisely, and have lost sight of what they have contracted you to do.

This is particularly true in situations where there are multiple stakeholders and you have been hired by one of them. You may find that to fulfil your remit you are working very closely with another of the stakeholders and are overempathizing with their needs and challenges. It's an easy trap to fall into, and even worse if it concerns an aspect of the project your client isn't connected with.

Always remember who is paying the bill.

MEASURE YOUR TIME

It is very common to put in more hours than you originally proposed – this means that the daily rate that you might have had to negotiate hard for could be reduced or even halved if you are not careful. Your client will be getting great value from you, but you will not be getting great value from them.

Whilst you are doing your work, keep a record of your hours and then at the end you can tally up how your hours worked compares with your proposal and agreed fee. There are a number of timesheet apps such as Toggl and HoursTracker that are designed to help you keep track of the hours you spend on different projects, but a simple spreadsheet or notebook will work just as well.

It's vital to get into the habit of recording the hours you work as it allows you to reflect back once the project is complete to see how realistic your proposal was and what you can learn from it for next time.

Overpromising and underdelivering is a sure-fire way to leave your reputation in tatters. But underpromising with the aim of overdelivering is likely to leave you without work as you haven't promised to deliver enough . . . It's a very fine line that only you can judge. But there are strategies to help you learn and adapt along the way.

WHAT'S WRONG WITH OVERDELIVERING?

Overdelivering is one of those things that seems like a good idea at the time. You think to yourself 'I'll quote the client for something that I think they'll buy and then I'll do a few more hours or days or I'll do a bit extra, just to show them how good I am and how much I want to work for them.'

Let's unpick this. You are offering to work for this client for some of the time for nothing. You are also offering the best bits of the work you do to them for nothing. You are not even telling them that you are doing this, so they have no sense of perceived value in this extra work you are doing.

There are two possible outcomes from overdelivering:

1. The client thinks you make a mountain out of a molehill with the work you deliver – it's much more than they asked for and they are unlikely to offer you further work.
2. The client loves what you've done and will hire you again, but on the same basis as they are getting super value from you.

Neither of these is the outcome you were looking to achieve. And remember, often the best way into a new client is to offer them something modest with a view to building a relationship and getting more work out of them. Overdelivering at the first point is not going to set your relationship up well and has the potential to do you out of work.

There is an alternative: selling whilst delivering.

SELLING WHILST DELIVERING

Selling whilst delivering is one of my favourite activities. It's where I'm at a client meeting on a project, which means I'm being paid to be there, and during this meeting I sell them another piece of work. Fantastic! I don't have to meet with the client speculatively (and in an unpaid capacity) to pitch and sell my services.

It works for the client too; they know I can deliver and they don't have to take the time to look for another freelancer, brief them and then get the project started. This is where the long-term value of the freelancer–client relationship starts to kick in.

Rather than overdelivering by throwing the next stage of the project that you could deliver into the mix for free early on, offer this as a next step or next project for the client as an outcome or recommendations from the work you are already doing.

This has many benefits; it demonstrates that you are thinking about the client and their needs, and you are giving reasons for them to work with you again in a situation where you can offer them further value. It can become a pattern. You do a piece of work for the client. At the end the recommendations include a further piece of work for them delivered by you. And so on. This won't apply to all clients and it won't be effective in all fields, but where you do get some traction it can be a great source of regular work.

I've had good runs with clients like this over the years but I'm always conscious that each project could be the last one. The client usually provides clues during the course of the work about whether there is more to come or not, so listen out for those. Listen out, too, for where their problem areas are – the chances are those need fixing and you might be able to offer a solution.

Some clients offer me a run of projects for six months, some for a few years. Some clients will book a regular piece of work once a year. Listening to your client and responding to what they are saying will help you decide how to build and develop a relationship that will allow you to keep selling whilst delivering.

INVOICING

After you've delivered your first piece of work to the client, all that remains is for you to be paid.

The only way to get paid for your services is to submit an invoice, so it's good practice to get into the habit of invoicing your clients promptly in accordance with the terms you've agreed. Legally, an invoice must contain the following (see sample invoice):

- The word 'invoice'.
- A unique identification number (invoice number) – it's a good idea to adopt a numerical system so that you can see at a glance which invoices have and haven't been paid. You could start 001, or some people prefer to identify the year as well 20–001. Then the next invoice is 20–002 then 20–003 etc.
- Your freelancer services name, address and contact information – this could be your own name or you may have given your services a trading name. You want to make sure you can be contacted easily in the event of any queries, so include your email and phone number as well as a postal address.
- The name and registered-office address of the client.
- The date of the invoice.
- A purchase order number, if given – many companies will send you a purchase order for your work, which needs to be quoted on your invoice or you may not get paid. Alternatively, you may have a contract, in which case reference this.
- The date the goods or services were delivered (supply date).
- A description of what you are charging for – make it something that is easily identified by the client; if your contract bore a description of the work, then use that.

- The amount(s) being charged net of any applicable taxes.
- If you are charging VAT or other sales tax then add in these details and the amount of the tax. You must also include your VAT or tax registration number.
- The total amount payable – if you don't charge VAT or sales tax this will be the same as the net amount above. If you do, it will be the total of the net amount plus tax.
- How the invoice should be paid. Usually, this means your bank details for monies to be credited to. If you are invoicing internationally you may need to add in the IBAN and Swift codes for your account.
- When the invoice should be paid. Don't forget to include a specific payment window, for example, 'Please pay within thirty days', not, 'Please pay as soon as possible'.

It's good practice to set up a template for your invoices containing all the standard details that are the same for every job. That way it is quick and easy to draw up a new invoice. If you have just a few regular clients, you can set up a Word or Excel template for each. There are also online systems linked to accounting software that can generate invoices for you. These can make invoices quicker and easier to send but are often generic and visually unappealing.

Your client's finance department will not drop everything to pay your invoice because you are desperate for cash and you've invoiced late. They will have a process and it will be paid according to that. Of course, if you have provided a reasonable deadline for payment that the client fails to meet, you can then legitimately describe your invoice as remaining unpaid when (politely) chasing the accounts department for payment.

Most companies require any invoice submitted to be in PDF format as such files cannot be amended post-submission. Attach your invoice to a covering email. This is usually addressed to the finance department with your client contact (who will have to authorize payment) copied in. The new-supplier forms you completed at the start should contain invoice instructions; if not, then ask before you send.

[Logo] [Freelancer Services Name] INVOICE

[Address]

INVOICE DATE: [insert date here]

INVOICE NUMBER: [no.]

ORDER NUMBER: [no.]

BILL TO: [Name]
[Company]
[Address]
[Address]
[Address]

BILL FOR: [service offered]

ITEM	NET	VAT or Sales Tax	TOTAL
[Detail supply dates here] [Detail services here]			
TOTAL			

TOTAL DUE: **[Amount]**

DUE BY: **[Date]**

BANK: [Bank name]

ACCOUNT NAME: [Account name]

SORT CODE: [Sort code]

ACCOUNT NUMBER: [Account number]

VAT NUMBER: [VAT no. if registered for VAT]

OUR TERMS ARE ____ DAYS FROM DATE OF INVOICE

[Insert Company Address Unique Taxpayer Reference (or company reg.no.)]

You've come a very long way and completed your first project. All that remains now is to record it in your system, but we'll come to that in the next chapter.

LEARNING BY EXPERIENCE

You've done the work; your invoice is in the system. It's tempting to move on straight away to the next commission as well as prospecting for more without reflecting back on how the job you have just finished went and whether you can learn anything from it.

Perhaps you've put in more hours than you expected and effectively sold yourself short. Now you are feeling resentful because the client expects you to price some more work at the same rate.

This isn't the client's fault, of course. The question now becomes how you can renegotiate the relationship to ensure you receive a fair price for the new work. (Don't fall into the trap of doing the same thing again and expecting a different result.)

This is where it helps if you have already taken charge of the communications with the client. If you've written up the proposal of the work to be done and stated the expected time and rate to be charged for this then you have a good starting position. Look at the expectations about rates and hours you set before you began the work – does this reflect how the actual work went? Did the client make unforeseen changes or steer the project in a new direction, meaning you had to work more hours than anticipated?

Before you respond to your client's new offer of work, take a moment to conduct a project reflection exercise. In the space provided, write on the left side the anticipated journey of the project from initial client contact to delivery (the project outline as per the original proposal) and then on the right-hand side map out the journey of the steps as they actually happened. You may need to look through your email or other correspondence with the client to remind you of the steps and communications involved as well as the log of hours you created as you worked on the project. Be really honest with yourself as you reflect on the journey.

This isn't the place to list the technical detail of the work, simply the steps and processes involved. By doing this you'll quickly get an idea how many steps were agreed and what the reality was. Equally, look at how much of your time was spent on the process of *managing* the project – in addition to doing the work you have expertise in. You should be paid for this too as it is part and parcel of delivering the work. It is also very common to overlook just how much time this takes up.

It's important to understand what happened. You can't change the past but you can learn from it and use this information to ensure that the next project you take on – with this client or with a different one – doesn't repeat the pattern. And if you didn't have a clear brief or proposal set out in the beginning you should now see the value in preparing one.

Compare both sides of the project reflection exercise to see if the left is sparser than the right. Ask yourself if this was a typical project. Were there were any mitigating factors that made this one more complex? Write them down. It could be the client was indecisive. If so, that's not your problem, it's the client's issue, so that should be a cost to them, not to you. Note these places.

Or perhaps you misunderstood a key detail or underestimated the amount of time required on the project when you submitted your proposal. If so, then that's your error and you need to think about why this happened and especially how you will avoid repeating this mistake. There is always a learning curve with a new client, and so also consider how much of this extra time you can attribute to this.

Now you are in a position to assess *why* it is that you worked so many more hours than you outlined in the original proposal. Think hard, too, about where during the project you've just completed there were warning signs that it was deviating from its intended track. Look back at your project reflection exercise and note down where in the process problems might have been anticipated. Now think back to whether you brought these to the attention of the

PROJECT REFLECTION EXERCISE

Project:	
Anticipated journey	Actual journey

client at the time and mark your sheet accordingly. Where you did address the signs, give yourself a pat on the back for tackling an issue within the project when it was current.

When you have completed the project reflection exercise and are ready to broach the subject with the client, take some time to consider what you want to say and how you want to say it. This is about more than just the money – it's about *educating the client about your value* so that they understand more about what it takes to do your work and the unintended consequences of changes made to the project along the way.

CUSTOMER FEEDBACK

It always surprises me how few freelancers ask for feedback at the end of a project. This is a valuable opportunity to learn from your work. Most clients are more than happy to give honest and constructive feedback. When you do ask, make sure you listen to what the client has to say. They will have a view of how the project went (and it can't have gone that badly if they want you to do more work). They will value being listened to, and this is really more about improving communication than about the quality of the work you have delivered. A key part of this conversation will be how you can communicate with each other during a project if it is going off course for either of you. This will mean that next time the brief changes you will have a plan of action to follow. This is a protection for both of you. Just make sure the conversation doesn't become personal.

You need to find a way to gently bring them round to your way of thinking. You don't want to overload them with too much technical information but you do need to find the path to constructive dialogue for future work. Find out what their expectations are. Where their pain is. You can often stumble across a bigger opportunity when you start probing where their pain points are.

If this looks like becoming a valuable client, think about how to build a long-term relationship with them. That is why these conversations are ideally done face-to-face, or at least over the phone. Email is a terribly blunt instrument for such conversations as it is so easily misconstrued and forwarded on. It should go without saying that any type of text message is not appropriate either.

As an illustration, go back to the first-date analogy. You're on your best behaviour and keen to impress whilst also trying to guess what the other person is thinking and assess whether they are good relationship material. It's hard work, and not always easy to let the real you shine through. If your first date goes well, then subsequent dates should become more relaxed as you get to know each other better and you can anticipate each other's likes and dislikes. You are in a similar position with this client. You've had a first date and things look promising, but there are a few areas you want to discuss before you are ready to go on another one.

It's far better to have clients with whom you can progress to a full relationship rather than being a serial first dater. New customers, like new partners, are costly to acquire in terms of both money and time. Think of all those meetings you went to *off the clock* and how long it took to prepare those proposals. You weren't paid for any of that. Now you are faced with a choice between re-educating a client you've already identified as having a budget and wanting more of your time or going out into the unknown. Put like that, it's a pretty simple decision.

None the less, you still need to decide up front what your walk-away point is. As part of this, consider whether you would do the work for them on the same terms as before or whether you would walk.

There are good reasons for both. You'll need to assess the wider picture of your work and whether taking what you are being offered is preferable to the alternative. This could be based on a need for cash, how valuable the profile of the client is to you, how worthwhile the experience they are offering is or if there is a good chance of better paying projects from them in the future.

You're not making a life commitment at this stage. If you do take another piece of work from them and are disappointed again then it will be your cue to walk. And beware of the client who dangles a bigger and better project under your nose as a carrot to get you to do this one on the cheap – not all of these carrots are edible.

GAINING TRACTION

Now that you've delivered your first piece of work and have more coming to fruition in your sales funnel, you must consider how best to pace yourself for the marathon you have just embarked upon.

13.

PACING YOURSELF FOR A MARATHON

You've done so much already, but this is only the beginning. Now it's time to become the multitasking juggler that is a fully fledged freelancer. I liken it to having to spin many plates and wear different hats simultaneously.

The spinning plates are all the different projects you are working on and have in the pipeline. The different hats are the different roles you have to play, over and above being the expert doing the work you do. As your portfolio builds and you take on more clients there are more people occupying the sales funnel, more work to deliver and more invoices and expenses to handle. This is where it is crucial to acknowledge the different hats you need to wear.

Each persona you adopt has its own role and scope of work necessary to ensure you are building a sustainable freelance existence. Four of the most important hats you wear (if you exclude making the tea) are those of chief executive officer (CEO), finance director (FD), marketing and sales director and chief operations officer (COO). Let's look at each of these roles more closely.

YOUR ROLE AS CEO

With your CEO hat on you need to be working *on* your freelance business as well as *in* it. This quote from Lewis Carroll's *Alice in Wonderland* is one I love as it cuts to the chase with no nonsense.

> Cat: Where are you going?
> Alice: Which way should I go?
> Cat: That depends on where you are going.
> Alice: I don't know.
> Cat: Then it doesn't matter which way you go.

Your CEO role is all about taking stock of

- Where you are at – *Am I offering the right services to my clients?*
- Where you'd like to get to – *How do I want my work to grow and develop?*
- Whether there are new opportunities to explore – *What is going on in my marketplace?*

And from that, planning how you are going to get to where you want to be. You are the one in the driving seat, so raising your head up and looking further down the road will help you to focus on targeting the work you want to win.

ARE YOU OFFERING THE RIGHT SERVICES TO YOUR CLIENTS?

If you are doing well at picking up new clients but not retaining them, what is the reason? Is it the nature of the services you offer? Are you selling something that people only ever need once? (A dating service is a good example of this: every time they're successful they lose two customers.) If so, then you need either more customers or a broader portfolio of services.

However, if you believe your customers could repurchase but don't, then think about your business process. It could be an indicator that your aim might be slightly off. If this happens, you need to examine why. At what point does the client decide that they will go elsewhere next time? Ask for feedback. Then try to understand what you can change to attract repeat business.

On the flipside, it's easy to fall into doing the work that clients want you to do, as opposed to the work that you find enjoyable, which isn't always the same thing. You're probably really good at it too, otherwise you wouldn't be offered so much of it. It may not be exactly what you thought you were signing up for by going freelance, but it pays the bills, so you go with the flow. The sheer fact that you are offered the work means that you are doing something right, but you should also consider whether you can improve your freelance experience by altering your offering to attract other work that you might be happier doing.

HOW DO YOU GROW AND DEVELOP YOUR WORK?

The regular work that clients book you for may be fine for now, but will it still be fine in three years' time? I try to find half a day every three months to spend a few hours in reflection, audit the work I've been doing and categorize it. This type of exercise is easy to put off, so set up a repeating reminder in your calendar.

I like to have three types of projects in play at any one time. The first are the 'low-hanging fruit'. This is the quick-turnaround, easy-to-pick-up work. The work you can do really well for clients. It isn't too taxing. It pays fairly well and allows time for other work.

The second type might be described as the 'middle-hanging fruit'. These are bigger projects, harder to get off the ground but ones that you have experience in. They are likely to be more challenging than the low-hanging fruit and take more time to ripen, but when they do, they are both more exciting and more rewarding.

The third and final type are 'speculative projects'. The ones that you'd really like to do but will take a lot of time and energy just to get to the starting line. They are often pet projects and labours of love when they first start but, tended well and with the right nourishment, can mature and provide significant rewards, both personal and monetary. They are the projects that take you to new places and push you outside your comfort zone.

If you focus solely on the easiest projects, you won't move towards your dreams. If you focus only on your dreams – the speculative projects – you are likely to go broke before you realize them. And doing only mid-range projects, although they'll keep you in work and your head comfortably above water, won't allow for your development.

That's why you should try to balance the three types at all times. However busy you are, you need to have strategies in play that will keep all three plates spinning. This doesn't mean you have to have all three types on the go at any one time, or even in any one week, but you should aim to include work on all three every month. If one type gets sidelined for a few weeks, be conscious of this and schedule some extra time to make up for the lack of attention you've given it.

Make an audit now of all the projects and clients you have in play currently. I call this the low-hanging-fruit exercise. Assign each one you are working on into a project type. If you are just starting

Low-Hanging Fruit Exercise

Low-hanging fruit	Middle-hanging fruit	Speculative projects

out and have few or no clients, use instead the types of client or project that you hope to secure. Ideally, your clients and projects should cover all three categories. If you feel any are over- or under-represented, it might be worthwhile adjusting your strategy.

With no employer to encourage your development in new areas and offer you coaching or mentoring, you have to do this for yourself. Working on speculative projects is a form of on-the-job training that allows you to push yourself in new areas and will also open doors that you might not otherwise have knocked on.

This book, for example, has been my biggest speculative project to date. Writing it hasn't been easy. I've had to put in a lot of hours, which has meant missing out in other areas of my life. But it has certainly opened new doors for me and is something I am really proud of.

Now that you know where you are at, it's time to look at where you want to get to. An exercise I find very helpful in quantifying this is something I call the letter-writing exercise.

Assume you are going to write a letter to an old friend to whom you haven't spoken in a couple of years, telling them what you've been up to recently. The twist is that you must date it *ten years* from today. This is a letter to your friend from your future self, so you need to decide who, what and where you plan to be in ten years' time.

To help you get started, first identify the person you might like to write to. And once you've done this, think about what you'd like to be able to tell them you've done in these last 'couple of years', i.e. eight to ten years ahead. Using a close friend as the addressee is important, as it will help you unlock your inner ambitions. You will find yourself wanting to tell your friend about your successes and the things you are proud of having done. From this you can start to identify where you want to be by then and build your strategy for getting there.

Once you've done this exercise, think about which of the projects you are working on are moving you in this direction. Be honest with yourself about which ones really are on target and focus your energy on landing more of these.

LETTER-WRITING EXERCISE

WHAT IS GOING ON IN YOUR MARKETPLACE?

The final part of the CEO role is keeping up with what is going on in your marketplace. That means staying abreast of new developments and changes both in your sector and in those sectors that impact your work. Keep up to date by reading relevant trade magazines and newsletters as well as attending events and conferences. It also means honing and improving your skills. Make sure you follow the action plan you devised in Chapter 2.

GOAL SETTING

As CEO, you now have all the information necessary to plan a route to your destination. You already have clear final goals from the letter-writing exercise; now break each one down into smaller, achievable milestones that will measure your progress along the way.

Be realistic. You know your marketplace is changing and therefore you may need to adjust or alter your goals or your pathways accordingly. Assess your progress during each of your quarterly reflection periods to make sure you are on track to reach them *and* that they are on track to satisfy you. Use a diagram like the one shown here to set your goals and then break them down into the steps you will take to achieve them.

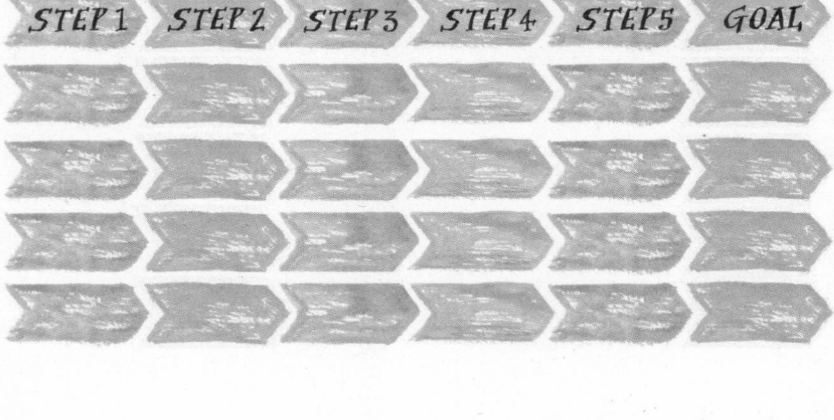

STEP 1 STEP 2 STEP 3 STEP 4 STEP 5 GOAL

YOUR ROLE AS FD

Alongside the CEO hat, the finance director's hat is likely to be the most time consuming to wear. The best way to minimize the pain is to keep on top of your finances each month and know when your filing deadlines are.

CASH FLOW

In your FD role you will be monitoring your cash flow – the money coming in and going out. Whilst your business account will tell you how much you have on hand at that moment, it doesn't tell you what is due to come in and what is due to go out. For this you need to keep your own records. It's best to align your records to your financial year. Start dates will vary according to your tax jurisdiction (some may be fixed and in others you may be able to choose), but every jurisdiction expects annual accounts to be filed and taxes to be paid, so keeping your records in such a way that they start afresh each financial year is good practice.

FILING ACCOUNTS AND TAX

Each year you (or your accountant) will need to file your accounts. These will cover the financial year just gone and will report the details of your income for the year and claim allowable expenses, tax allowances and tax reliefs in accordance with the regulations wherever you are filing. From them, you or your accountant can calculate your taxes owing for the year.

RECORD KEEPING

Keeping good records is vital, not just to provide you with the information you need to prepare regulatory paperwork but also to understand your business and how it's performing. At the very least you need to keep an up-to-date record of all the money coming in and all the money going out. This can be as simple as a spreadsheet with a worksheet for revenues and a worksheet for expenses.

Alternatively, there are many software packages available for accounting and/or receipt keeping that can do this for you, such as FreeAgent or Xero, plus the fintechs, such as Coconut who offer an automated function. Remember, they don't keep records by magic; you do need to input the information. The best way to do this is to set aside an hour or so each week to update all the expenditure on the business and to prepare any invoices. You don't want to end up with a year's worth of receipts and other paperwork to write up and only a few days to do it in.

Record keeping divides into two basic areas: income and expenditure.

INCOME

Every invoice you raise should be entered into your spreadsheet with details of the date raised, the amount invoiced, the invoice number and payment status on one worksheet. Many accounting packages have built-in invoicing software which can do this tracking for you.

For logistical reasons I like to include the client details as well, though this isn't strictly necessary. I also like to keep track of pending work that might be about to land as well as confirmed work. This gives me an at-a-glance picture of what I've received, what's due to come in and what might come in.

A simple income spreadsheet

Invoice Date	Details	Paid	Invoiced	To invoice	Possible	Invoice no.
1 Jan. 20	Company A		£1000			001
March	Company A			£1500		
5 Jan. 20	Company B	£300				002
12 Jan. 20	Company C			£240		003
February	Company D				£500	
TOTAL		**£300**	**£1000**	**£1740**	**£500**	

Once the work is confirmed and I've invoiced, I'll move that figure across to the Invoiced column and add in the invoice number and date. Once the invoice has been paid, I move it across to the Paid column. A simple spreadsheet such as this gives you at a glance the total possible turnover you have in the pipeline for the current financial year.

Every time an invoice is paid, transfer a proportion of this money into your business savings account to cover your tax liability. Your accountant can advise you what proportion is advisable in your jurisdiction. (In the UK a good rule of thumb is 25 per cent.) I had a nasty surprise once when I didn't have enough put aside due to lack of self-discipline – though it has to be said I do still wear the boots I used the money for! Seriously, not a good strategy. Trust me.

EXPENDITURE

As well as your income you need to keep records of your business expenditure – the date of purchase, who you purchased from, how much it was – and give it what accountants call a 'code', in other words, a category or bucket that you can lump all similar expenditure into so that at the end of the year you can see how much you've spent in each area.

By using your business bank account for all your incidental business costs – train fares to meetings, stationery, research materials and any other solely business-related purchases – you can keep track very easily of all your expenses. Most business bank accounts give you the option to download your statements into a format such as .csv that you can open in Microsoft Excel and manipulate so that it's quick and easy to pull your expenditure together for the year ready for your accounts to be prepared.

There are no specific requirements for expenditure codes, or for how many you should use. Ten or twelve is a good working number; any more gets rather unwieldy and creates too much overlap. A typical set might be: Your wages; Travel; Subsistence; Equipment; Research Materials; Office Costs; IT; Marketing; Bank charges;

Accountancy; Legal fees; and Insurance. You'll have to work out for your business which specific ones make the most sense to you.

As in many other areas of work, technology is coming to our aid with programs and apps that can help keep records, track expenditure and do invoicing. They come pre-loaded with standard setups, which are a good starting point. Some can even scan your receipts and do most of the hard work for you, such as 1tap receipts or Receipts by Wave. Saviour or gimmick? It's up to you to do your research and see what can be of genuine help to you.

Whatever system you use it is solely your responsibility to keep records of your business activities and the associated receipts. Your accountant may process them for you, but if you make a mistake then it's you who will carry the can.

If you pass on a project's expenses to the client, these will show as both expenditure and income on your records (expenses because you have paid for them but income because the company will have reimbursed you). If they are for the same amount (i.e. you have not applied a mark-up), they will cancel each other out and will have no effect on your tax position, but you still need to record them.

GETTING PAID

With your FD hat on you are also going to need to keep track of what you are owed and when it is due. Building a good relationship with your clients' finance personnel can go a long way to ensuring you are paid on time.

Each company will have its own system for paying invoices. It is good practice to make yourself aware of what they are: how to address your invoice, where to send it and whether there are cut-off days each week or month by which you need to invoice in order to be paid quickly.

If you don't get paid on time, politely nudge the finance department to find out where your invoice is in their system. They will be able to advise you when you can expect payment or tell you if it has not yet been passed for payment. If the latter, then get in touch with your client contact to ascertain what the problem is and resolve it. They are usually keen to know if there are issues their end with payments to suppliers.

You will most likely receive a profuse apology and prompt payment, but if this doesn't happen then it's time to send a firm reminder to both your contact and the finance department, explaining that the invoice is now overdue for no legitimate reason and that if they don't settle within a specified period (e.g. fourteen days) you will levy late-payment charges in accordance with your terms and conditions of business. (If you don't have terms and conditions of business then you can't say you do in your letter.)

If the invoice is still unpaid after this period then send a final demand. Write again, this time expressing disappointment that they haven't paid and outline the amount owing, any late payment charges and interest levied, and again request payment within a specified period (e.g. fourteen days), once more in line with your terms and conditions.

Follow each of these stages up with a phone call. As a last resort, you might need to take legal advice on how to claim an unpaid debt.

PAYING THE BILLS

Alongside collecting the money you are owed you also need to pay your debts. As mentioned, I try to pay for any business-related items using my business bank account. When it comes to paying for services that I hire in I like to adopt a 'do as you would be done by' approach and pay as soon as the invoice has landed. I know my subcontractors appreciate it, and it's less work for me as I don't have to remember to do it later. It's just done. The subcontractor is happy and so am I.

PENSIONS

Pensions are long-term investments that you put money into each month, typically into funds that buy bonds or shares with the aim of growing your pot exponentially over the years. Small regular contributions over a long period have the potential to grow significantly, depending on financial market conditions. It's surprising how even a tiny amount put away each month can add up over time.

Planning your pension becomes a challenge when cash flow is irregular as it can be hard to commit to a regular amount of money to lock away. Financial advisers will tell you that you can't start pension planning early enough.

When it comes to choosing a pension there are a vast array of products and it can be hard to work out what is the right one for you. Additionally, it's common when you first start freelancing to consider it a temporary arrangement, so you don't look into it. Then you get busy, embark on a freelance career and still don't look into it. This is where a qualified financial adviser can help you navigate the many options in the market, pull together any pension(s) you may already have and work out what you can afford to set aside – this could be in the form of a monthly payment as well as an annual top-up, which you could save for by setting aside a percentage of your income in the same manner as you do for your tax bill.

YOUR ROLE AS MARKETING AND SALES DIRECTOR

With your marketing and sales director's hat on you will be keeping your sales funnel filled and moving. If it's looking a little empty, work harder on topping it up. If it's looking full then work harder on moving clients through the funnel.

Also, give your old clients a tickle, and by this I don't mean ask for work – send them something interesting you think they'd like to know. If you assume your clients like your work and would give you more if they could, then keeping in touch with them regularly can be a good strategy. It goes back to the Dunbar number. Each of your clients has 150 people in their network that they could refer you to; that's a lot of potential people you could be recommended to. It pays to remind your network of your existence.

It's very easy, particularly when you are busy in paid work, to slacken off or cease your marketing and sales activity. Then you get to the end of the busy paid period and find your sales funnel is empty and you need to start from scratch building it up. That's fine if your finances allow for extended dry spells. If they don't then you need to carve out time in your diary to keep your potential sales moving. Use the database you created to help with your client prospecting. This needn't take long: as little as fifteen minutes per day can make a difference. You can also do blog posts and social media updates that talk interestingly about the work you are doing.

YOUR ROLE AS COO

In your role as chief operating officer you are first and foremost scheduling your work to ensure that you deliver to your clients on time, but it is also where you make sure you carve out the time in your diary to wear your other hats and that you keep working *on* your business as well as *in* it.

The COO looks ahead to the forthcoming day, week, month and year, examines workload and deadlines and schedules work accordingly. The COO part of you also has to assess whether you have the capacity to deliver a new project in the timescale the client wishes.

A simple starting point is a calendar on which you input all the key deadlines that you have coming up, both for your client-paid work and for the work of your other hats. If you do this on your computer you can also schedule reminders for your deadlines to prompt you to get the work done in a timely fashion.

Some freelancers I know like to detail each day precisely and block out time for each client. Others take a more laissez-faire approach with just the headlines. There's no right or wrong way, only the way that works for you. What I can say for sure is that taking time to plan your days, weeks and months will make it much easier to wear all your hats and keep your plates spinning.

As you gain experience and take on bigger clients and projects you will need to consider how you price your time. You can make the best use of it by focussing on delivering the work you do well that adds the most value and outsourcing the more routine operations, thereby freeing you up to go after more value-added work.

A COO also has to deal with the difficult stuff, such as when a project goes wrong or life throws you a curve ball. Integrity, honesty and realism will get you through. Even the toughest of clients is a human being underneath. People make mistakes. Things don't go according to plan. That's a given. What *is* in your control is how you deal with it.

Despite the best intentions, something will usually go wrong at some point. When this happens, honesty is always the best policy. I've seen freelancers try to brush mistakes under the carpet and hope they won't come to light. They always do. It's like secrets – they have a way of getting out.

Facing up to the situation and communicating early with the client is your best option, even if it doesn't feel like it at the time. Rather than panic, take stock of where you are at, work out what possible routes forward there are, then inform your client in a calm and considered fashion, explaining what's happened and how you see the way ahead. This is the sort of conversation that's best had face to face with a client or on the phone. It's probably not best done by email – although that's a good way to prime someone in general terms before the main conversation so they don't get too nasty a surprise.

At the meeting, if the client becomes angry, stay calm and keep the conversation focussed on potential solutions. This isn't the time for an inquest, that can come later; the priority is to get the project back on track and that's where solutions come in.

Some of the best client–freelancer relationships I've ever had have been the product of adversity. The freelance administrator I hired at Girls Angels pitched me a proposal for her services after our systems failed her and she arrived to take her bike test without the relevant paperwork. Completely our fault. As the consummate freelancer, she saw her opportunity to fix this and make sure it didn't happen again.

The same is true when something happens unexpectedly that forces you to take time out from your client work. Give your clients as much notice as you can. You'll be surprised how well people respond. Be honest and realistic in what you can (or can't) now do. Any client who responds badly to this sort of news is probably not one you want in the longer term, so take the stress out of your life and drop them.

Being a freelancer is definitely a marathon rather than a sprint, so treat it as such. Dashing away from the start line won't build you a sustainable freelance career. Investing time in your clients and your freelance business will reap rewards. Just remember to invest time in yourself too. You are your business; if you aren't in good shape then neither is your business.

LOOK AFTER NUMBER ONE

It's easy enough to promise to look after yourself, get plenty of rest, take time out, but when you are in the thick of it, it can be much easier said than done. No one can give 100 per cent every day to everyone. At some point, something has to give. So pace yourself; understand when you are reaching your limits. Indulge in a little you-time. You will perform much better if you are fit, both mentally and physically, so place a high value on looking after yourself.

If I'm having a particularly taxing day, I'll take a thirty-minute walk for a change of scenery. It helps me relax and process what's going on. Some people go to the gym, some read, some like to cook. It doesn't matter what form your safety valve takes. What matters is that you are valuing yourself and your state of mind, and taking the time to keep them in shape.

Not only is it important to take short breaks when you need them during your working week, you also need to build in time off over the year. *Real* time off, not time out from the paid work to get your finances in order or do some marketing. Aim to keep your weekends free to enjoy with friends and family and schedule in holidays for proper downtime. That's why you wanted to be a freelancer after all.

Value your time and spend it wisely.

AND FINALLY . . .

I know freelancing isn't for everyone, but it can be a fantastic life once you embrace it. I've written this book to assist you in becoming the best freelancer you can be.

You know you've got the talent to do the work; this book is here to help you improve those aspects of freelancing you don't do quite so well so you can provide a better service and get more of the work you love from the clients you really want to be working with.

This is a great time to be a freelancer, so get out there, grab the work and enjoy yourself.

APPENDICES: LEGAL, INSURANCE, HEALTH AND SAFETY

First, an important disclaimer. This book is intended to provide you with the tools to turn your passion into a business or career and is based on my real-life experience of doing just that – as well as many lessons I've learned from others. I'm neither a lawyer nor an accountant (although I have paid a few in my time!) and nothing in this book is intended to constitute legal or financial advice or to substitute for the opinion of a suitably qualified professional who understands your circumstances. This section in particular is nothing more than an illustration of the principal areas in which you might need to seek professional guidance.

LEGAL

From a legal perspective there are three main areas that every freelancer needs to be aware of (plus there may be additional requirements specific to the sector you work in). These are

- terms and conditions;
- intellectual property;
- non-disclosure agreements.

TERMS AND CONDITIONS

Your terms and conditions cover the small print common to every job and set out in legal terms what you expect from a client when you work with them. They should be attached to every proposal and invoice you send to a client. Whilst the majority of the time you won't pay much attention to your terms and conditions once they are written, they are essential if a client relationship breaks down as it will be these that are scrutinized to understand the legal basis of your dispute.

You can hire a solicitor to write them for you, although this can be quite expensive. Many trade associations and professional bodies that support freelancers also offer legal-services support and templates that do the same job – probably for less money and more upside as you will be part of a community of like-minded freelancers.

INTELLECTUAL PROPERTY

Intellectual property (IP) refers to creations of the mind, such as inventions; literary and artistic works; designs; and symbols, names and images used in commerce. It is protected by law through patents, copyright and trademarks.

An example of IP creation is when you hire a photographer for a photoshoot. The photographer will own the copyright in the photos they take. You will need to license or be assigned the copyright in the photos in return for an agreed sum, in addition to the photographer's fee for taking the photos.

If your work involves IP creation then you must be clear in your pricing, terms and conditions and communications with clients what they are buying and where the ownership will lie at the conclusion of the agreement. For example, if you are a graphic designer and you are engaged to design a company's new logo for their business, they are going to require that the logo designs you create for them during this process are fully assigned to them worldwide in perpetuity. It is their brand, after all; however, you may wish to charge them accordingly.

NON-DISCLOSURE AGREEMENTS

A non-disclosure agreement (NDA) – sometimes referred to as a confidentiality agreement – is a legal agreement between two or more parties that outlines confidential information they wish to exchange for the purposes of working together, or when considering working together. It creates a duty of confidence to protect trade secrets or confidential or proprietary information not in the public domain.

You are most likely to come across them when a client or potential client needs to share confidential or otherwise sensitive information about a project with you and wants to ensure that information does not leak. They need to specify what is confidential and there are restrictions – for example, if the information is already in the public domain or gets there and didn't come from you, you're fine. Also, NDAs can't be used to conceal criminal acts.

They are pretty standard in their terms – just remember that if you are subcontracting work, your subcontractors need to sign an NDA too. A word of warning: if an NDA appears too restrictive, wide-ranging or onerous, seek legal advice before you sign.

PROFESSIONAL BODIES

A professional body is an organization of people with a common interest. They charge an annual subscription and provide a range of services to their members. These will usually include lobbying government on their behalf, regular newsletters and events, plus legal support and contract services. Some professional bodies are standards based and some aren't.

In the UK IPSE (The Association of Independent Professionals and the Self-Employed) is the largest membership body that represents freelancers. In the USA the Freelancers Union promotes the interests of independent workers.

INSURANCE

There are four key areas here to consider – but again there may be more depending on the type of work you do. The four main areas are:

- public liability;
- professional indemnity;
- equipment/office contents;
- employer's liability.

As well as these you also need to consider how freelancing might affect your personal insurance (e.g. life or accident cover) and your motor policy. It's worth doing some research here as costs can vary widely. There are providers who specialize in freelancer insurance, such as GetDinghy in the UK and the Freelancers Union in partnership with Hiscox in the USA.

PUBLIC LIABILITY INSURANCE

This is often required by clients and proof may be requested as part of contract negotiations. Public liability insurance protects you if clients or members of the public suffer personal injury or property damage because of your business. It can pay for the costs of subsequent legal expenses or compensation claims and is an integral cover for businesses that interact regularly with customers.

The minimum level of cover usually offered in the UK is £1 million but some larger companies and institutions may ask for higher cover. You will need to think about the types of customers you are working with and assess your levels of cover accordingly.

PROFESSIONAL INDEMNITY INSURANCE

This is an important cover if you give advice or provide a professional service to clients. It can pay for compensation claims and legal fees that may arise if a client suffers a financial or professional loss due to negligence in your work – be that advice, services or designs. More specifically, professional indemnity insurance covers you for mistakes such as professional negligence, unintentional breaches of copyright or confidentiality, loss of documents or data, defamation or libel.

Even if you've done nothing wrong, the cost of defending yourself against these claims can be very high. Professional indemnity cover can help protect you against this risk.

EQUIPMENT/OFFICE COSTS

If you work from home, don't assume that your personal household insurance will cover your equipment and your office. Typically, cover will depend on the use of the home being for clerical purposes only (i.e. office work), and you may not be covered if you have any business visitors. If you work from home, the best thing to do first is to talk to your current insurer and explain your situation. They might ask for an additional premium on your current insurance. If you don't tell your insurers and you need to make a claim, you might find that your insurance is invalid and that the claim won't be paid.

Additionally, if you have specialist items of equipment you use to deliver your services you may find these hard to add to your home insurance policy, and should you suffer a loss or breakdown you may find that your home insurance cover doesn't allow you to get up and running again as quickly as you would like, in which case specific business insurance may be preferable.

EMPLOYER'S LIABILITY INSURANCE

Employer's liability insurance protects you against the cost of compensation claims arising from employee illness or injury sustained as a result of their work for you. If you employ people, then you are legally required to buy this cover. It is also worth checking with your insurer about hiring freelancers as, depending on the work they do for you, you may need to cover them.

PERSONAL INSURANCE

In addition to your business insurances you may also want to consider personal insurance options as well, including:

- Income protection – designed to provide financial support if you are unable to work due to accident or sickness. It will usually pay a fixed amount per month until you return to work, subject to a maximum period (e.g. twelve months or two years).
- Critical illness cover – long-term cover that will provide a lump sum if you are diagnosed with a critical illness.
- Life insurance – designed to pay out a lump sum should you pass away during the term of the contract.
- Private medical insurance – cover designed to meet some or all of the costs of private medical treatment for certain conditions.

Everyone's requirements and circumstances are unique, so consult a qualified professional.

MOTOR INSURANCE

Don't assume that your domestic motor policy will automatically cover you for your freelance operations. You must ensure you have appropriate cover for your vehicle for the work that you do.

There are different levels of business cover and you should choose the most appropriate for your needs. If you drive your car for business purposes only infrequently, a policy that covers private and occasional business use will probably be adequate. Private and business use is a step up and is aimed at people who regularly drive their car for business. Then there's commercial car insurance, which is for people who rely on their car for their business, such as a courier or a private-hire vehicle.

If you carry equipment or tools in your vehicle, make sure you understand the conditions of cover. Some insurers will not cover your equipment, others will impose a claim limit. There will almost certainly be a raft of exclusions, so make sure you are aware of them and adhere to any conditions.

HEALTH AND SAFETY

If you are self-employed, work alone and your work activity poses no potential risk to the health and safety of other workers or members of the public you are unlikely to come under health-and-safety legislation. Otherwise, the regulations will apply to you. As always, seek professional advice if you are unsure.

A 'risk' to the health and safety of others in the workplace means the likelihood of someone else being harmed or injured as a consequence of your work activity. You must consider the work you are doing and judge for yourself if it creates a risk to others or not. If you believe it does, then it is your responsibility to take appropriate steps to minimize or eliminate any risk to others.

Many people use the terms 'hazard' and 'risk' interchangeably. They are very different. For example a shark in an aquarium is a hazard. It's only a risk if you decide to swim in the tank with it.

It is good practice when working in another company's premises to provide evidence of your public liability insurance. In addition, you should also make yourself aware of their health-and-safety policy and ensure your work complies with it.

If you do believe there is a risk to the health and safety of others you should conduct a risk assessment.

RISK ASSESSMENTS

A risk assessment is a tool to help you manage your safety and the safety of others. The aim is to prevent injury and illness through proper planning. Part of that planning will be the arrangements needed to deal with emergencies, including serious and imminent danger. There are five basic steps to preparing a risk assessment:

1. Identify the associated hazards.
2. Decide who might be harmed and how.
3. Assess the level of risk.

4. Formulate the control measures needed, put them in place and tell the people affected.
5. Monitor the work to make sure that the assessment remains valid.

Risk assessment of any action/activity relies on the competence and experience of those individuals evaluating and supervising it. If such people are not already part of your core team then you will need to contract them in (examples in the film industry might include stunts, special effects, filming on water etc.) and have them supply their own supplementary risk assessment.

WITH THANKS TO . . .

All the freelancers I have had the pleasure of working with as a team member, trainer or mentor over the years.

My first boss, the late Ivan Rendall, my first mentor and one of the wisest people I've had the pleasure of working for.

Mike Southon, my mentor and friend, who supported me at the start of my entrepreneurial journey and asked the difficult but obvious questions.

Percy Emmett, who trained me to be a Nesta Creative Enterprise facilitator and the angels I trained with.

Sara Middleton, associate dean at Birmingham City University, who hired me as a consultant for a project during which time I had the idea for this book.

The lunch crew at the Old Print Works, for keeping me sane during the early stages of writing when it was still a speculative project.

To Joanna Birch, Debbie Boucher, Jonathan Carpenter, Noel Dunne, Jane Gill, Charlotte Heather, Vicky Jepson, Mike Johnson, Rozanna Josef Drago, Karen Kamel, Lee Kemp, Tim Kevan, Richard Leeming, Gemma Long, Shalini Marimuthu, Annette Naudin, Maria Needle, Sam O'Connor, Caroline Officer, Hayley Pepler, Vicky Peters, James Poole, Carl Reader, Johnny Rickard, Drew Roper, Sarah Rutter, Esther Shaylor, Marc Silk, Helen Spencer, John Spencer, Susanna Stanford, Shigeri Takamatsu, Samantha Thodhlana, Cathryn Thompson-Goodwin, Gillie Traeger, Ben Wilks and John Wyver, for wittingly and unwittingly contributing.

To my mother and Max, for their unending support and encouragement. To my father and Francesca, for their unshakeable belief in me as an author. And particularly, to my boys, Thomas and Alex, who put up with me on a daily basis and allowed me to disappear for entire weekends so I could make this happen.

This book would not be the book it is today without four specific people. William Gallagher, who urged and supported me to get writing and was there when I needed a cup of tea and a pep talk. Martina O'Sullivan and Celia Buzuk at Penguin, who believed in me and this book from our first meeting and whose expertise and advice has challenged and developed my thinking, and my husband, Seán, who was there all the way through as a sounding board and a sense checker.

INDEX

Page references in *italics* indicate images or tables.

PENGUIN PARTNERSHIPS

Penguin Partnerships is the Creative Sales and Promotions team at Penguin Random House. We have a long history of working with clients on a wide variety of briefs, specializing in brand promotions, bespoke publishing and retail exclusives, plus corporate, entertainment and media partnerships.

We can respond quickly to briefs and specialize in repurposing books and content for sales promotions, for use as incentives and retail exclusives as well as creating content for new books in collaboration with our partners as part of branded book relationships.

Equally if you'd simply like to buy a bulk quantity of one of our existing books at a special discount, we can help with that too. Our books can make excellent corporate or employee gifts.

Special editions, including personalized covers, excerpts of existing books or books with corporate logos can be created in large quantities for special needs.

We can work within your budget to deliver whatever you want, however you want it.

For more information, please contact
salesenquiries@penguinrandomhouse.co.uk